THE A KU-414-474

Until her tragically early death in October 1982, Marika Hanbury Tenison was one of Britain's leading writers on food and cookery. She was for fourteen years cookery editor of the *Sunday Telegraph* and wrote over twenty-five cookery books. She won the André Simon Award in 1980 and was 1981 Corning Food Writer of the Year.

Marika was particularly well qualified to write on fish, being Deputy Chairman of the Sea Fish Industry Authority. She has written a companion Sainsbury's Food Guide, *Buying and Cooking Fish and Seafood*, on all aspects of choosing, preparing and cooking fish. In this new edition of *The Fish Recipe Book* some recipes which had to be omitted previously, through lack of space, have been included.

INTRODUCTION

Why cook fish? The answer, quite simply, is that it makes good sense to have at least one fish dish, and even as many as two or three, each week. It makes sense because fish is not only delicious but also the purest, cleanest and most healthy food available to twentieth-century man. Compared to other protein foods such as meat it is good value for money; there is little wastage and it is quick to cook and simple to prepare.

Fish is a very versatile food, and to prove it I have provided in this book a range of recipes which vary from the very simple to the ultimate in sophistication. Cooking should be fun, not a chore. Because it can be quickly cooked and because of its comparatively delicate flavours, fish responds well to being served with sauces and in made-up dishes, although often it can also be quickly grilled or fried.

From the simple fried fillet served with lemon wedges and an interesting sauce to a more exotic recipe of mixed seafood in light, mouthwatering pancakes, fish in one form or another makes an unbeatable basis for a vast range of family and dinner-party meals.

Garnishes

Although I have made specific suggestions in many of the recipes, garnishing is very much a matter of taste and the choice of garnishes for fish is wide. The following ideas may be helpful.

Anchovies A naturally 'fishy' accompaniment and garnish for fish dishes. Drain canned anchovies of their oil and cut them lengthways into strips before using them as a garnish for hot or cold dishes.

Breadcrumbs Many hot fish dishes in sauces call for a final covering of breadcrumbs and a quick crisping under the grill. Make fresh white or brown breadcrumbs from 2–3-day-old stale bread by rubbing it through a coarse grater, or

Note on quantities

Ingredients in the recipes are given in both imperial (oz, pints, etc) and metric (g, ml, etc) measures: use either set of quantities, but not a mixture of both, in any one recipe. All spoons are level unless otherwise stated; metric spoon measures are always level. Egg size, where unspecified, is medium (size 3).

4

A SAINSBURY COOKBOOK

THE
FISH RECIPE BOOK

MARIKA
HANBURY TENISON

CONTENTS

Published exclusively for J Sainsbury plc
Stamford House Stamford Street
London SE1 9LL
by Martin Books
Simon & Schuster International Group
Fitzwilliam House 32 Trumpington Street
Cambridge CB2 1QY

First published 1983
New enlarged edition 1985
Fourth impression 1990

Text, photographs and illustrations
© J Sainsbury plc 1985, 1990

ISBN 0 85941 538 4

Printed in Great Britain

whizz up fresh breadcrumbs in seconds in an electric liquidiser or food processor.

To make home-made dried breadcrumbs for toppings or for coating fish, dry slices of stale bread in a low oven until crisp and golden. Leave to cool and then crush into small crumbs with a rolling pin or in a liquidiser or food processor.

Cucumber   Cucumber is a natural partner to a dish of cold salmon and is also useful to add to baked fish dishes, as well as to incorporate into a pretty, cool and dainty sauce for summer fish dishes. To prevent too much liquid seeping from the cucumber, slice or dice it, place it in a colander or sieve, sprinkle with salt and leave to stand for 30 minutes to 'sweat'. Shake off excess water and pat dry on kitchen towelling.

Deep-fried parsley   Crisp, crunchy, deep-fried parsley sprigs are a delight as a garnish for any fried fish and especially for whole fried fish like whitebait and sprats. Remove any tough stalks from the sprigs; do not wash unless absolutely necessary and, if you do, dry the sprigs really well in plenty of kitchen paper. Fry in really hot, deep oil (watch for spitting) for about 5 minutes until they are crisp, curled and crunchy. Drain on kitchen towelling.

Lemon   Most fish benefits from the addition of lemon juice. Serve fried, poached and baked fish, especially oily fish like mackerel and herring, with slices of halved lemons with the pips removed. An attractive idea for a party is the Italian custom of wrapping lemon halves in circles of butter muslin tied at the top, so that guests can squeeze the lemon without getting any pips on their fish.

Prawns   Whole prawns in their shells make a delightful garnish for both hot and cold fish dishes. You only need a few ounces, or a handful, to hang over the side of a fish cocktail or to decorate a fish salad or hot fish dish at the last minute.

Tomatoes   Tomatoes are one of the most natural accompaniments to fish. Serve grilled halved tomatoes with hot dishes and garnish cold ones with sliced or 'water-lily' tomatoes.

FISH STOCK

1 large onion, peeled and sliced

2 sticks of celery, chopped roughly

2 carrots, peeled and sliced

1½ teaspoons (3 × 2.5 ml spoon) mixed herbs

2 cloves

12 peppercorns

2 bay leaves

6 sprigs of parsley

1½ tablespoons (4 × 5 ml spoon) salt

2 lb (900 g) fish bones, heads, etc.

3 pints (1.8 litres) water

I have written in more detail about the various types of fish, and how to prepare and cook them, in Sainsbury's Food Guide No. 12, *Buying and Cooking Fish and Seafood*. Information about basic sauces, etc., can be found there, although you do not need it in order to make the recipes in this book, which are entirely self-contained. The following basic recipe for a fish stock (properly called a fish fumet) will, however, be found useful for some of the dishes in the book.

Combine all the ingredients in a large pan, bring to a vigorous boil and then simmer, covered, for 1 hour. Strain the liquid before using.

   Note: when using fish fumet for a sauce, reduce it by at least a third by boiling rapidly before use.

PREPARING FISH AND SEAFOOD

Scaling a fish
If sea bass, carp, grey mullet, salmon or sea trout are to be cooked with the skin on, remove the scales first under cold running water by scraping with a sharp knife.

Preparing a lobster
Use a sharp, thick-bladed knife to separate the two halves of a lobster from head to tail. The small sac and the black tail vein, highlighted in the diagram, should be removed. All other parts, including the roe and the greenish substance near the head, are edible (and delicious). The claws and legs should be cracked with a large nutcracker to remove the meat.

Preparing fresh scampi
Cut the underside of the shell with scissors and carefully lift out the tail, removing the brown gut.

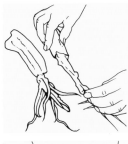 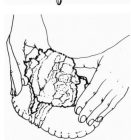  

Preparing a crab
Twist off the claws and legs, crack with a nutcracker and remove the white meat to a bowl. Push back the pointed flap curving under the body and press the body out of the shell. Remove and discard the white, feathery 'fingers' and the transparent stomach sac. Scoop out the brown meat into a second bowl. Break the body into four and with a skewer pick out all the white meat, adding it to the meat in the first bowl.

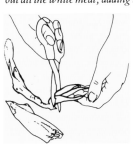 

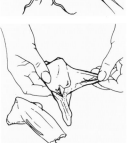

Preparing a squid
Pull off the head and tentacles and cut off the head behind the eye, leaving the tentacles intact. Pull out the plastic-looking gristle from inside the squid and wash out the body sac. Wash and dry the body and tentacles and chop up the latter. Peel the outer skin from the body and chop the body into rings.

*White Fish and Scallop
Terrine
Crab and French Bean
Salad
Prawn and Rice Salad*

8

PRAWN AND RICE SALAD

12 oz (350 g) long grain or
patna rice

¼ pint (150 ml) olive or
sunflower oil

1 tablespoon (15 ml spoon)
lemon juice

½ teaspoon (2.5 ml spoon)
mixed herbs

2 spring onions

1 green pepper

2 tomatoes

8 oz (225 g) peeled prawns
or 8 scampi

salt and freshly ground black
pepper

To garnish:

2 teaspoons (2 × 5 ml
spoon) finely chopped
parsley

*This makes a lovely salad to serve as a main course for
a summer lunch.*

Cook the rice in boiling, salted water until just
tender. Drain, rinse in a sieve in cold running
water and shake well to remove excess water.
Combine the oil and lemon juice, add the herbs
and season with salt and pepper; mix this
dressing into the rice while it is still warm. Leave
to cool.

Trim and chop the spring onions finely.
Remove the core and seeds from the green
pepper and chop the flesh. Cover the tomatoes
with boiling water for 30 seconds, drain and
slide off the skins; remove the cores and seeds
and chop the flesh. Shell the scampi, if used, and
cut each into three pieces. Crack the claws and
remove the flesh.

Add the prawns or scampi, spring onions,
pepper and tomatoes to the rice and mix the
ingredients. Pile on to a serving dish and dust
with the parsley. Serve with crisp french bread
and a mixed or green salad.

CRAB AND FRENCH BEAN SALAD

8 oz (225 g) young french beans

2 firm, ripe tomatoes

3 spring onions

2 hard-boiled eggs

3 tablespoons (3 × 15 ml spoon) olive or sunflower oil

1 tablespoon (15 ml spoon) white wine vinegar

½ teaspoon (2.5 ml spoon) Dijon mustard

a few drops each of Worcestershire and Tabasco sauces

1 tablespoon (15 ml spoon) tomato ketchup

1 crisp lettuce, shredded roughly

½ cucumber, cut into thin 2-inch (5 cm) sticks

8 oz (225 g) white crab meat

salt and freshly ground black pepper

To garnish:

6 black olives

Make this in the spring or early summer when french beans are small and tender.

Top and tail the beans and cook them in boiling, salted water for about 6 minutes until just tender. Drain and rinse at once in cold running water and pat dry on kitchen towelling. Cover the tomatoes with boiling water for 30 seconds, drain and slide off the skins; slice the flesh thickly. Trim the spring onions and cut into four lengthways. Shell and quarter the hard-boiled eggs.

Combine the oil, vinegar, mustard, sauces and tomato ketchup in a screw-topped jar, season with salt and pepper and shake well to mix. Arrange the lettuce in a shallow serving dish and place the cucumber, tomatoes, egg quarters and spring onions around the outside. Pile the beans in the centre and spread the crab over the beans. Pour over the dressing, garnish with the olives and serve chilled with crisp french bread.

WHITE FISH AND SCALLOP TERRINE

Serves 6

8 oz (225 g) haddock fillets with the skin removed (you can also use cod, hake or whiting fillets)

2 oz (50 g) fresh white breadcrumbs

milk

2 eggs

1 oz (25 g) cottage cheese

1 tablespoon (15 ml spoon) double cream

1 tablespoon (15 ml spoon) finely chopped chives

a pinch of mixed herbs

1 lb (450 g) spinach

3 scallops

salt and freshly ground black pepper

a pinch of ground nutmeg and cayenne

Oven temperature:
Gas Mark 4/350°F/180°C

A pretty green terrine with a layer of scallops in the centre. Try serving it with a spicy tomato sauce.

Mince the fish through a fine mincer or food processor. Soften the breadcrumbs in milk, squeeze out the excess milk and add the crumbs to the fish. Beat the eggs lightly and the cottage cheese until smooth (both best done in the liquidiser or food processor). Gradually mix the egg, cottage cheese and cream into the fish, beating or processing until the mixture is smooth. Add the chives and mixed herbs and season with salt, pepper, nutmeg and cayenne.

Preheat the oven. Pick over and wash and dry the spinach leaves and blanch them for 3 minutes in boiling salted water. Drain well and press out all the excess moisture. Very finely chop or purée, add to the fish mixture and mix well. Remove the corals from the scallops and discard any black vein and muscle. Slice the white part.

Line a 1½-pint (900 ml) terrine with lightly oiled foil. Spread half the fish mixture in the terrine and top with the sliced scallops and the corals. Cover with the remaining fish mixture, pressing it down firmly. Cover the terrine tightly with foil and place it in a bain marie or roasting dish with enough boiling water to come half-way up the side of the terrine. Bake in the oven for 1 hour.

Remove the terrine from the bain marie and leave to cool. Unmould and refrigerate until well chilled. Serve cut into thin slices and with a sauce of your choice.

FRIDAY SOUP

Basic stock: Fish stock, page 6

1 oz (25 g) butter

4 onions, sliced thinly into rings

2½ pints (1.5 litres) fish stock, or water and 2–3 chicken stock cubes

a few drops of Worcestershire sauce

1 tablespoon (15 ml spoon) chopped parsley

¼ teaspoon (1.25 ml spoon) mixed herbs

4 tablespoons (4 × 15 ml spoon) white wine

1 lb (450 g) fish fillets (use any firm white fish or lemon sole), cut into bite-size pieces

5–6 × 3-inch (8 cm) diameter circles of french bread, buttered

1 clove of garlic, crushed

1 teaspoon (5 ml spoon) made English mustard

1½ oz (40 g) grated Gruyère or Emmenthal cheese

salt and black pepper

Oven temperature:
Gas Mark 8/450°F/230°C

A classic French onion soup is delicious and nutritious (and an excellent cure for a hangover!); add fish to that and you have a hearty meal in its own right.

Preheat the oven. Melt the butter in a saucepan, add the onion rings and cook over a *low* heat (do not allow to burn) until the onions are golden and soft and the butter has been absorbed. Add the stock, Worcestershire sauce, parsley and mixed herbs, season with salt and pepper and simmer for 20 minutes to develop the onion flavour. Add the wine to the soup, put in the fish and cook over a low heat, at simmering point, for about 3 minutes until the fish is just tender.

Spread the buttered circles of bread lightly with the garlic and mustard and press on the grated cheese. Brown in the oven for 5 minutes until the cheese has melted and is golden and bubbling. Ladle the soup into hot bowls and float the cheesy toast on top before serving.

Serve the soup with extra french bread on the side and follow it with a fruit bowl and you have a first-rate inexpensive supper.

CREAM OF CRAB SOUP

Basic stock: Fish stock, page 6

3 oz (75 g) butter

1 onion, peeled and chopped finely

2 carrots, peeled and chopped finely

2 stalks of celery, chopped finely

2 tablespoons (2 × 15 ml spoon) tomato purée

2 pints (1.2 litres) fish stock, or water and 2 chicken stock cubes

1 lb (450 g) crab meat, half white and half brown

1 teaspoon (5 ml spoon) Dijon mustard

3 fl oz (90 ml) medium sherry

5 fl oz (150 ml) carton of double cream

2 teaspoons (2 × 5 ml spoon) brandy

salt and freshly ground black pepper

a pinch of ground nutmeg

A delicious and sophisticated soup to start off a dinner party.

Melt the butter in a large saucepan. Add the onion, carrot and celery and cook over a low heat, stirring to prevent browning, until the vegetables are soft. Add the tomato purée and mix well. Gradually blend in the stock, bring to the boil and boil over a high heat for approximately 15 minutes until the liquid is reduced by about a quarter.

Add the white crab meat, mustard and sherry, season with salt and pepper and a pinch of nutmeg and simmer for 10 minutes.

Strain off and reserve the liquid and purée the vegetables and crab meat through a fine sieve, or in a liquidiser or food processor. Return the purée to a clean pan with the cooking liquid, brown crab meat and cream and heat through until very hot. Check the seasoning and pour into heated serving bowls, pouring a little brandy over the top of each bowl just before serving.

HADDOCK AND CHEDDAR SOUP

Serves 4–5

Basic stock: Fish stock, page 6

1 lb (450 g) haddock fillet or other firm-fleshed white fish fillet

1½ oz (40 g) butter

1 large onion, peeled and chopped finely

1 large carrot, peeled and chopped finely

2 sticks of celery, chopped finely

4 tablespoons (4 × 15 ml spoon) plain flour

1¾ pints (1 litre) fish stock, or water and a chicken stock cube

3½ oz (90 g) mild Cheddar cheese, grated

salt and freshly ground black pepper

To garnish:

1½ tablespoons (4 × 5 ml spoon) finely chopped parsley

A hearty warming and nourishing soup for a winter or cold autumn evening. Hake or coley can be used in place of the haddock.

Steam the fish in a colander or steamer over simmering water until just tender; then allow to cool. When cool, remove any skin and bones and flake the flesh.

Melt the butter in a large saucepan. Add the chopped vegetables and cook over a low heat, stirring, until they are soft. Add the flour and mix well. Gradually add the stock, stirring continuously over a medium–high heat until the mixture comes to the boil and is smooth. Simmer for 5 minutes, or until the vegetables are tender, and season with salt and pepper.

Add the fish and simmer for 3 minutes. Stir in the cheese over a low heat, stirring until it has melted; do not boil or the soup may curdle. Sprinkle over the parsley and serve.

CELERY AND SMOKED HADDOCK SOUP

12 oz (350 g) smoked haddock

¾ pint (450 ml) milk

¼ pint (150 ml) water

8 oz (225 g) firm-fleshed white fish, with skin and bones removed

2 oz (50 g) butter

1 large onion, peeled and chopped finely

2 sticks of celery, sliced thinly

1½ tablespoons (4 × 5 ml spoon) plain flour

2 bay leaves

5 fl oz (150 ml) carton of single cream

2 tablespoons (2 × 15 ml spoon) finely chopped parsley

freshly ground black pepper

Place the haddock in a shallow pan, pour over the milk and water, season with pepper, bring gently to the boil and simmer for 5 minutes. Strain off and reserve the cooking liquid, remove any remaining skin and bones and flake the flesh. Cut the white fish into small cubes.

Melt the butter in a saucepan, add the onion and celery and cook over a low heat, stirring, until the onion is soft and transparent. Add the flour and mix well. Gradually blend in the reserved cooking liquid, stirring continually, over a medium–high heat until the liquid comes to the boil and is smooth. Simmer for 10 minutes, stirring occasionally, and then add the white fish, haddock and bay leaves and simmer gently for a further 10 minutes. Remove the bay leaves, stir in the cream and parsley and heat through without boiling.

Celery and Smoked Haddock Soup

WEST COAST SALAD

2 lb (900 g) mussels

3 tablespoons (3 × 15 ml spoon) dry white wine

1 small lobster, cooked

8 scampi, cooked

3 small, ripe tomatoes

6 tablespoons (6 × 15 ml spoon) olive or sunflower oil

3 tablespoons (3 × 15 ml spoon) lemon juice

½ teaspoon (2.5 ml spoon) Dijon mustard

1 teaspoon (5 ml spoon) each finely chopped chives and parsley

2 crisp lettuce hearts, shredded roughly

½ cucumber, cut into thin 2-inch (5 cm) sticks

4 oz (100 g) firm button mushrooms, sliced

salt and freshly ground black pepper

A really luxurious dish that is the shellfish equivalent of a grand 'Chef's Salad'. Serve the salad as the centre-piece of a summer buffet or lunch party. It looks best in a large glass bowl if you have one.

Scrub the mussels under cold running water, removing any barnacles with a knife. Remove the wiry beards protruding from the shells. Place the mussels in a large, heavy saucepan, pour over the wine, cover tightly and cook over a high heat, shaking the pan now and then, for 6 minutes until the mussels have opened (discard any that don't). Drain off, strain and reserve a little of the liquid and leave the mussels to cool. When cool, remove them from their shells.

Halve the lobster lengthways with a sharp knife, discard the black vein and stomach sac and remove all the meat from the body. Crack the lobster claws with a hammer or nutcrackers and remove all the meat; cut it into ¾-inch (2 cm) cubes. Remove any meat from the legs. Peel the scampi tails and crack the claws to remove any meat. Cover the tomatoes with boiling water for 30 seconds, drain and slide off the skins; quarter the flesh.

Combine the oil, lemon juice and mustard in a screw-topped jar with 1 tablespoon (15 ml spoon) of the liquid in which the mussels were cooked and season with salt and pepper. Add the chives and parsley and shake well to mix. Arrange the lettuce in a large bowl. Arrange the tomato quarters and cucumber sticks around the outside and pile the lobster, scampi, mussels and sliced mushrooms in the centre. Pour over the dressing and serve well chilled with boiled new potatoes or a potato salad.

WEST INDIAN FISH SALAD

1½ lb (675 g) firm white fish (try haddock, hake or cod)

1 tablespoon (15 ml spoon) olive or sunflower oil

2 teaspoons (2 × 5 ml spoon) curry powder

1 small paw-paw

2 tablespoons (2 × 15 ml spoon) flaked almonds

1 tablespoon (15 ml spoon) mango chutney, chopped finely

½ pint (300 ml) lemon mayonnaise

2 sticks of celery, chopped finely

½ crisp lettuce, shredded

1 teaspoon (5 ml spoon) lemon juice

Oven temperature:
Gas Mark 6/400°F/200°C

An attractive summer dish for serving on a warm day.

Place the fish in a lightly buttered steamer and steam over boiling water for about 10 minutes or until the fish is just cooked and the flesh will flake. Cool, remove the skin and divide the fish into large flakes.

Preheat the oven. Heat the oil in a small pan, add the curry powder and stir over a low heat for 2 minutes to soften the powder and release its flavours. Peel and halve the paw-paw and remove the seeds. Cut the halves into ¼ inch (5 mm) thick slices. Roast the almonds in the oven for 2–2½ minutes until golden brown, and then cool.

Add the curry mixture and mango chutney to the mayonnaise and mix well. Fold in the fish and the celery. Arrange a bed of lettuce in the centre of an oval serving dish, pile the fish mayonnaise on the top and surround with the paw-paw slices brushed with a little lemon juice. Sprinkle the almonds over the top of the fish.

NORTH SEA FISH CHOWDER

Basic stock: Fish stock, page 6

2 small onions

1–1¼ lb (450–550 g) potatoes

2½ pints (1.5 litres) fish stock, or water and 2–3 chicken stock cubes

2 rashers of fat, streaky bacon, with the rinds removed

2 carrots

8 oz (225 g) firm white fish (e.g., coley, cod, halibut or conger eel), off the bone with the skin removed

½ tablespoon (3 × 2.5 ml spoon) sunflower oil

½ teaspoon (2.5 ml spoon) turmeric

¼ teaspoon (1.25 ml spoon) fines herbes

4 tablespoons (4 × 15 ml spoon) single cream

salt and pepper

Chowder is the American term for a fish soup that is thick, creamy and richly nourishing. It can be a main course in its own right, served with crisp french bread and butter.

Peel and chop the onions finely. Peel half the potatoes and cut them into small neat dice. Peel and boil the remaining potatoes and mash them with a little of the stock until smooth and creamy. Dice the bacon. Peel or scrape and grate the carrots coarsely. Cut the fish into small cubes.

Heat the oil in a saucepan. Add the bacon and cook, stirring, over a medium–low heat for 2 minutes. Add the onion and potato cubes and stir over a medium heat for about 5 minutes until all the fat is absorbed. Add the stock, season with salt and pepper, mix in the turmeric and herbs and stir well. Bring to the boil and simmer for 15 minutes.

Mix in the mashed potato and carrot, stirring until the soup is thick, and then add the fish. Simmer gently for about 5 minutes or until the potato cubes and fish are tender. Add the cream, check the seasoning and serve very hot.

Note: you can add a little white wine in place of some stock and you can garnish the soup with some finely chopped parsley at the last minute.

North Sea Fish Chowder
Pickled Herrings

PICKLED HERRINGS

1 orange

8 herring fillets

¼ pint (150 ml) white wine vinegar

8 peppercorns

1 onion, peeled and sliced

4 bay leaves

¼ pint (150 ml) water

salt

Oven temperature:
Gas Mark 5/375°F/190°C

Serve with a mixed salad and crisp french bread to make a summer lunch dish.

Preheat the oven. Remove the orange rind very thinly, with a potato peeler, and cut into very thin julienne strips. Squeeze out the juice and put on one side. Roll up the herrings with the skin side out and secure with cocktail sticks. Place the herrings in a lightly oiled baking dish just large enough to accommodate them. Pour over the orange juice and vinegar, sprinkle over the orange rind strips and some salt and add the peppercorns. Top with the sliced onion and bay leaves and pour over the water (there should be enough liquid to cover the fish). Cover tightly with foil and bake in the oven for 30 minutes.

Leave the fish to cool in the cooking liquid and then chill in a refrigerator. Drain the fish and remove the cocktail sticks before serving.

SALMON AND CELERY REMOULADE

Serves 4 as a starter or 2 as a main course

1 small head of celery

1 teaspoon (5 ml spoon) lemon juice

2 salmon steaks

court bouillon (see below) or chicken stock

1 tablespoon (15 ml spoon) olive or sunflower oil

1 teaspoon (5 ml spoon) Dijon mustard

¼ pint (150 ml) mayonnaise

4 tablespoons (4 × 15 ml spoon) double cream

salt

cayenne pepper, to garnish

Simple court bouillon mixture:

1½ pints (900 ml) cold water

1½ tablespoons (4 × 5 ml spoon) white wine vinegar

1 carrot, sliced

1 onion, peeled and sliced

bouquet garni

6 black peppercorns, crushed

1 teaspoon (5 ml spoon) salt

Remove the leaves and any tough fibres from the celery and cut the stalks into 2-inch (5 cm) lengths and then into very thin matchstick strips. Add the lemon juice to a pan of boiling, salted water and cook the celery in it for 6 minutes until tender but still crisp. Drain, rinse in cold running water and pat dry on kitchen paper.

Place the salmon steaks in a shallow pan and add enough cold court bouillon or chicken stock to cover; add the oil and bring slowly to the boil. Remove from the heat and leave to cool in the cooking liquid. Drain off the liquid, remove the skin and bones from the fish and coarsely flake the flesh.

Add the mustard to the mayonnaise and mix well. Whip the cream until thick and fold into the mayonnaise, add the salmon and celery and mix lightly. Pile on to a serving dish, sprinkle with a little cayenne pepper and serve chilled.

SMOKED SALMON ROLLS WITH ARBROATH SMOKIE MOUSSE

2 Arbroath smokies

¼ pint (150 ml) double cream

1 teaspoon (5 ml spoon) horseradish sauce

2 teaspoons (2 × 5 ml spoon) lemon juice

¼ pint (150 ml) mayonnaise

8 thin slices of smoked salmon

salt and freshly ground black pepper

To garnish:

4 large crisp lettuce leaves

4 wafer-thin slices of lemon and a little cayenne pepper

Arbroath smokies are small haddock or whiting which have been cured in brine and smoked. As they do not keep for very long, do not buy them more than two days before making this recipe.

Remove all the skin and bones from the smokies and flake the flesh. Whip the cream until thick and light. Add the horseradish sauce and lemon juice to the mayonnaise, season with salt and pepper and fold the whipped cream into the mayonnaise mixture together with the flaked smokies.

Spread out the smoked salmon slices and divide the mousse mixture between the slices, turn in the ends and roll up lightly into long parcels. Arrange these parcels on the lettuce leaves, sprinkle with a little cayenne pepper and garnish with the slices of lemon. Serve well chilled with slices of buttered brown bread.

Smoked Salmon Rolls with Arbroath Smokie Mousse
Marinated Kipper Salad

MARINATED KIPPER SALAD

3 kipper fillets

4 tablespoons (4 × 15 ml spoon) olive or sunflower oil

1 tablespoon (15 ml spoon) lemon juice

1 teaspoon (5 ml spoon) crushed coriander seeds

2 firm, crisp eating apples

8 oz (225 g) cooked new potatoes

2 spring onions

1 small green pepper

freshly ground black pepper

To garnish:

crisp lettuce leaves

½ tablespoon (3 × 2.5 ml spoon) finely chopped parsley

lemon wedges

Serve as a first course or a light lunch in summer.

Remove the skin from the kipper fillets and cut the flesh into ¼-inch (5 mm) strips, across the grain. Place in a shallow dish. Mix the oil with the lemon juice and season with pepper and crushed coriander. Pour over the fish and refrigerate for 3 hours, stirring every now and then.

Peel and core the apples and cut them into small dice. Cut the potatoes into small dice. Trim the spring onions and slice thinly. Remove the core and seeds from the green pepper and chop the flesh. Add the apples, potatoes, spring onions and pepper to the fish and marinade and toss the ingredients lightly together.

Pile the salad on to crisp lettuce leaves on four plates and sprinkle over the parsley. Serve with wedges of lemon on the side, accompanied by slices of buttered brown bread.

KIPPER AND MUSHROOM PÂTÉ

Serves 6

2 pairs of kippers

5 oz (150 g) butter

2 oz (50 g) firm button mushrooms, sliced

juice of ½ lemon and the finely grated rind of ¼ lemon

7 fl oz (210 ml) double cream

1½ oz (40 g) clarified butter (butter melted and passed through a fine sieve)

freshly ground black pepper

a pinch of ground nutmeg and cayenne

Oven temperature:
Gas Mark 5/375°F/190°C

Heat the oven. Place the kippers in a baking dish, dot with 1 oz (25 g) of the butter cut into small pieces and cover with foil. Bake in the oven for 20 minutes until the flesh will flake. Drain off and reserve the juices from the dish. Remove the skin and bones from the kippers.

Put the juices from the kippers in a small saucepan, add the mushrooms and toss over a high heat for 2 minutes. Drain off and reserve the cooking juices and leave to cool.

Soften the remaining butter and blend with the kipper fillets, cooking juices, lemon juice and rind in a liquidiser or food processor; season with freshly ground black pepper and the ground nutmeg and cayenne pepper. Continue to process until the ingredients are reduced to a smooth paste.

Whip the cream until light but not thick. Fold the mushrooms and then the cream into the kipper pâté and divide it between six small pots. Pour a thin layer of clarified butter over each pot and chill in the refrigerator for at least 1 hour. Serve the pâté with lemon wedges on the side and with hot triangles of toasted bread.

CURRIED FISH COCKTAIL WITH POPPADUMS

½ large cucumber

8 oz (225 g) white fish fillets (e.g., haddock or hake)

2 tablespoons (2 × 15 ml spoon) double cream

6 fl oz (175 ml) mayonnaise

1 teaspoon (5 ml spoon) curry paste

1 teaspoon (5 ml spoon) lemon juice

1 small dill pickled cucumber, chopped finely

1 crisp eating apple, peeled, cored and chopped finely

6 poppadums

oil for frying

4 oz (100 g) peeled prawns

salt

To garnish:

12 mint leaves

Peel the cucumber, cut in half lengthways, scoop out and discard the seeds and cut the flesh into small dice. Put the diced cucumber in a sieve or colander, sprinkle with salt and leave for about 30 minutes. Then pat dry with kitchen towelling to remove excess liquid.

Steam the fish in a lightly buttered steamer or colander over boiling water for about 6 minutes until the fish is just tender. Leave to cool and then flake the fish. Add the cream to the mayonnaise with the curry paste and lemon juice and mix well.

Fold the fish, dill pickled cucumber, apple and diced cucumber into the curried mayonnaise, mix lightly and chill until ready to serve. Fry the poppadums in a little hot oil, pressing down to flatten them and turning them once until they are crisp. Leave to cool and drain on kitchen paper.

When ready to serve, place the poppadums on six serving plates, half cover with the fish mayonnaise, top with the prawns and garnish with the mint leaves. Serve at once.

Grilled Scampi
Curried Fish Cocktail with Poppadums

GRILLED SCAMPI

12 scampi in their shells

4 tablespoons (4 × 15 ml spoon) olive or sunflower oil

1 tablespoon (15 ml spoon) lemon juice

2 cloves of garlic, peeled and crushed

1 teaspoon (5 ml spoon) mixed herbs

a few drops each of Worcestershire and Tabasco sauces

salt and freshly ground black pepper

To serve:

lemon wedges and mayonnaise

Place each scampi on a chopping board covered with a damp cloth and cut neatly with a sharp-pointed knife down the centre of the back. Remove any black veins and stomach sacs from the scampi and arrange them cut side up in a grill pan.

Combine the oil with the lemon juice, season with salt and pepper and mix in the garlic, herbs and a few drops of each of the sauces. Pour this sauce over the scampi and grill about 3 inches (8 cm) away from the heat, basting with any juices from the pan for about 10 minutes until the scampi are hot through and golden on top. Serve at once with wedges of lemon and a bowl of mayonnaise on the side.

MARINATED SALMON

1 lb (450 g) salmon, off the bone with the skin removed

1 onion, peeled and sliced into rings

1 tablespoon (15 ml spoon) coriander seeds, crushed

juice of 1 lemon

4 tablespoons (4 × 15 ml spoon) olive or sunflower oil

dry white wine

salt and freshly ground black pepper

To garnish:

lettuce leaves

In this unusual first course the fish is 'cooked' in a marinade of lemon juice, wine and oil. The resulting salmon is rich and succulent and has a delicious flavour.

Cut the salmon across the grain into ¼ inch (5 mm) thick slices; cut the slices into strips about 2 inches (5 cm) long and ¼ inch (5 mm) wide and arrange them closely, but not quite touching, in a single layer in a shallow dish. Season the strips with salt and freshly ground black pepper, spread the onion rings over them and sprinkle over the crushed coriander seeds. Pour over the lemon juice and the oil and enough white wine just to come over the top of the fish. Refrigerate for 4 hours until the fish is beginning to turn opaque around the edges.

Remove the onion rings, lift the strips of fish from the marinade, brushing off any of the coriander, and arrange them on lettuce leaves on individual plates. Serve chilled with slices of buttered brown bread.

HEARTY HADDOCK, POTATO AND LEEK SOUP

Serves 4

1 lb (450 g) potatoes

3 small leeks

1 Finnan haddock, or 12 oz (350 g) smoked haddock or cod

2½ oz (65 g) butter

½ pint (300 ml) milk

1½ pints (900 ml) fish or chicken stock, or water and stock cubes

freshly ground black pepper

To garnish:

1 tablespoon (15 ml spoon) finely chopped parsley

Oven temperature:
Gas Mark 6/400°F/200°C

Soups like this can be almost a main course in their own right. Try serving this for a winter lunch with plenty of crusty french bread and you will see what I mean. All you need to follow is a bowl of fresh fruit and some cheese.

Peel the potatoes and cut them into small dice. Clean and thinly slice the leeks, including a good proportion of the green tops. Preheat the oven.

Butter a shallow baking dish, put in the fish, dot with ¾ oz (20 g) of the butter, pour over the milk and bake the fish in the oven for 10 minutes, until the fish will just flake. Remove the fish from the milk and carefully remove the skin and any bones. Reserve the cooking liquid.

Melt the remaining butter in a heavy saucepan and add the potatoes; cook over a low heat, stirring, for 5 minutes. Add the leeks and stir over a low heat until they are soft and all the butter has been absorbed. Add the reserved cooking liquid from the haddock, bring to the boil and boil gently until the potatoes are tender. Add the stock, season with pepper, mix in the fish and heat through. Sprinkle over the parsley just before serving.

Note: for special occasions whip 3 fl oz (90 ml) double cream until thick, pour the soup into heated bowls and add a spoonful of whipped cream as you serve the soup. The parsley can be sprinkled over the cream.

MAIN COURSES

Chinese Fried Cabbage with Bacon, Leeks and Scallops
Fillets of Sole with Lemon Sauce and Herbs
Catalan Fish Parcels

33

CHINESE FRIED CABBAGE WITH BACON, LEEKS AND SCALLOPS

Serves 4

3 large scallops

1 small or ½ large savoy or white cabbage

oil for deep frying

3 rashers of streaky bacon, with rinds removed and chopped finely

1 oz (25 g) butter

3 cloves of garlic, peeled and chopped finely

3 leeks, cleaned and sliced thinly

juice of ½ large lemon

salt and freshly ground black pepper

For this dish I use a combination of crisply fried cabbage strands cooked Chinese style to surround a continental-type dish of scallops and bacon. The resulting mixture of the crisp and the softly flavoursome is a good contrast in texture. Take care when cooking the cabbage as the shredded leaves tend to spit when they are lowered into the hot oil.

Remove the pink coral from the scallops, remove any tough fibre from the side of the white part and pull off any black veins; thinly slice the white part. Cut out the core of the cabbage and shred the leaves very finely, drying them thoroughly on kitchen towelling.

Heat the oil in a large pan. Put the cabbage in the oil carefully and fry until crisp and lightly browned. Remove with a slotted spoon and drain well on kitchen towelling. Make a border of the fried cabbage around a shallow serving dish and keep warm.

Put the bacon in a heavy frying pan and cook over a low heat until the fat runs out and the bacon is crisp. Add the butter to the bacon and the juices in the pan and put in the garlic and leeks. Cook over a medium heat, stirring to prevent sticking, until the leeks are soft. Add the scallops, season with salt and pepper, mix in the lemon juice and cook over a low heat, stirring occasionally, for 2 minutes. Add the scallop corals and toss over a medium–high heat for a further minute. Turn the scallops and leek mixture into the centre of the crisply fried cabbage and serve at once, perhaps with Savoury Rice (page 44).

CATALAN FISH PARCELS

1 large, ripe, firm tomato

1 large banana

oil

4 thick cutlets of white fish (use sea bass, haddock, hake or cod)

4 thin slices of lemon and 1 teaspoon (5 ml spoon) lemon juice

a pinch of mixed herbs

1½ oz (40 g) butter

salt and freshly ground black pepper

Oven temperature:
Gas Mark 6/400°F/200°C

These are savoury and aromatic fish steaks wrapped in foil and baked in the oven. The fish can be served in the 'parcels' or you may prefer to remove it from the foil, arrange it on a serving dish and pour over the juices from the parcels.

Cover the tomato with boiling water, leave to stand for about 1 minute and then drain and slide off the skin. Quarter the tomato, remove the core and seeds and finely chop the flesh. Peel and slice the banana. Preheat the oven.

Oil four pieces of foil, each about 10 × 8 inches (25 × 20 cm), and place a fish cutlet in the centre of each piece. Season the fish with salt and pepper and place a slice of lemon on each cutlet. Top with the slices of banana and then with the tomato, sprinkle over the lemon juice and the mixed herbs and season with a little extra salt and pepper. Dot with small pieces of the butter and draw the foil up loosely over the filling, twisting the edges to seal the parcels.

Place the parcels on a baking sheet and bake in the oven for 30 minutes.

Serve with mashed or new potatoes and a green vegetable.

FILLETS OF SOLE WITH LEMON SAUCE AND HERBS

4 large or 8 small fillets of lemon sole, with the black skin removed

plain flour

1 small lemon

3 oz (75 g) butter

8 tablespoons (8 × 15 ml spoon) chicken stock (or use water and ½ stock cube)

6 tablespoons (6 × 15 ml spoon) dry vermouth

2 tablespoons (2 × 15 ml spoon) finely chopped chives (or spring onion tops)

1 tablespoon (15 ml spoon) finely chopped parsley

a pinch of dried sage

salt and freshly ground black pepper

A delicately sharp little dish that makes an excellent main course for a summer meal.

Coat the fish fillets in flour seasoned with salt and pepper. Cut the lemon in half lengthways and then into the thinnest possible slices, removing the pips.

Heat the butter in a large frying pan until foaming. Add the fish and cook over a medium-high heat for about 3 minutes each side until the fish is just cooked through. Remove the fish to a heated serving dish and keep warm.

Add the stock and vermouth to the juices in the pan, scraping the pan well. Bring to the boil and cook over a high heat until the liquid is reduced to about a third. Add the herbs and lemon slices, season with extra salt and pepper if necessary and simmer for 3 minutes. Arrange the lemon slices on the fish and pour over the sauce from the pan. Serve at once with boiled new potatoes, mashed potatoes or Savoury Rice (page 44) and accompany with a green vegetable such as cabbage, spring greens, spinach or leeks.

SOLE VERONIQUE

dry white wine

8 oz (225 g) green grapes

4 large or 8 small fillets of
flat fish with the black skin
removed (use Dover or
lemon sole)

water

2 sprigs of parsley

1 small onion, peeled and
sliced thinly

1½ oz (40 g) butter

1½ tablespoons (4 × 5 ml
spoon) plain flour

¼ pint (150 ml) double
cream

¼ teaspoon (1.25 ml
spoon) dried tarragon

1½ tablespoons (4 × 5 ml
spoon) finely grated
parmesan cheese

salt, freshly ground black
pepper and ground nutmeg

*One of the most subtle and delicious of classic fish
dishes. You* must *peel the grapes, otherwise the
texture of the dish will be spoiled.*

Heat a little wine and blanch the grapes in it for a
few minutes. Then slide off the skins and halve
the grapes, removing the pips.

Place the fillets in a large, heavy frying pan
and pour over enough white wine and water, in
equal quantities, to cover them. Season with
salt, add the parsley and onion, bring slowly to
the boil and cook for about 5 minutes until the
fish is just tender. Remove the fish with a slotted
spoon to a heated serving dish and keep warm.

Strain the cooking liquid into a saucepan,
bring to the boil and boil over a high heat until
the liquid is reduced to about 8 fl oz (240 ml).
Melt the butter in a saucepan, add the flour and
mix well. Gradually blend in the cooking liquid,
stirring continuously, over a medium-high heat,
followed by the cream, until the sauce comes to
the boil and is thick and smooth. Add the
tarragon and peeled grapes and season with salt,
pepper and nutmeg. Pour the sauce over the fish,
sprinkle over the parmesan and brown quickly
under a hot grill.

Serve with mashed or new potatoes and
spinach or some other green vegetable.

SQUID PROVENÇALE

1 lb (450 g) squid

lemon juice

4 medium-size tomatoes

2 tablespoons (2 × 15 ml spoon) olive or sunflower oil

2 large onions, peeled and chopped very finely

2 cloves of garlic, peeled and chopped very finely

1 tablespoon (15 ml spoon) tomato purée

¼ pint (150 ml) red wine

a pinch each of oregano and thyme

1 tablespoon (15 ml spoon) finely chopped parsley

salt and freshly ground black pepper

A rich and aromatic stew of squid and tomatoes with herbs.

To clean the squid, pull off the head and tentacles and cut off the head behind the eyes, leaving the tentacles intact. Pull out the plastic-looking backbone from the inside of the body sac and wash the sac well, removing any soft white substance from inside. Peel off the outer, purplish skin from the body and fins of the squid. Cut the squid body into thin rings and chop the tentacles. Sprinkle with lemon juice and season with salt and pepper. Cover the tomatoes with boiling water, leave to stand for 30 seconds and then drain and slide off the skins; discard the cores and seeds and chop the flesh.

Heat the oil in a saucepan, add the onion and garlic and cook over a low heat, stirring to prevent sticking, until the onion is soft and transparent. Add the squid and mix well. Add the tomatoes, tomato purée and red wine, bring to the boil and cook over a high heat for 5 minutes to reduce the wine. Add enough water to cover the ingredients, season with salt and pepper, mix in the herbs and simmer gently without covering for about 40 minutes until the sauce is thick and the squid is tender. Serve with rice and a mixed salad.

FISH STEAKS WITH MUSTARD SAUCE

Serves 4

4 white fish steaks
(haddock, pollock or cod)

1 teaspoon (5 ml spoon)
lemon juice

6 tablespoons (6 × 15 ml
spoon) plain flour

3 oz (75 g) butter

½ pint (300 ml) milk

1 tablespoon (15 ml spoon)
Dijon mustard

1 tablespoon (15 ml spoon)
finely chopped parsley

salt and freshly ground black
pepper

Mustard is a classic accompaniment to fish, and very good it is, too.

Sprinkle the fish with the lemon juice. Coat the fish with 2 tablespoons (2 × 15 ml spoon) flour, seasoned with salt and pepper. Place the fish in a lightly buttered grill pan with the rack removed and dot with 1 oz (25 g) of the butter. Grill under a medium heat for about 6 minutes on each side until just cooked through. Remove and keep warm.

Melt the remaining butter in a saucepan, add the remaining flour and mix well. Gradually blend in the milk, stirring continuously, over a medium–high heat until the sauce comes to the boil and is thick and smooth. Add the mustard, season with salt and pepper, stir in the parsley and heat through. Pour the sauce over the fish and serve at once.

Note: one tablespoon of milk can be replaced by a tablespoon of dry vermouth.

CRISP CHEESY FISH STRIPS

Serves 4

1 lb (450 g) white fish fillets

7 tablespoons (7 × 15 ml
spoon) golden breadcrumbs

½ oz (15 g) grated
parmesan cheese

1 large egg (size 1–2),
beaten

oil for deep frying

salt and freshly ground black
pepper

To garnish:

lemon wedges

A variation on the 'goujons' theme with the addition of a grated parmesan coating which makes a quick method of cooking inexpensive fish such as small whiting, haddock or hake fillets.

Cut the fish into thin diagonal strips (the size of your little finger). Combine the breadcrumbs and parmesan cheese and season with salt and pepper. Dip the fish in the egg and then coat in the breadcrumb mixture. Heat the oil until hot enough for deep frying, add the fish a handful at a time and cook until crisp and golden brown. Drain well on kitchen towelling and serve piled on a white napkin with a garnish of lemon wedges.

TROUT WITH ALMONDS

4 trout, approx. 8 oz (225 g)
each, cleaned and gutted

plain flour, seasoned with
salt and pepper

sunflower oil

2 oz (50 g) butter

3 oz (75 g) flaked almonds

juice of ½ lemon

salt and freshly ground black
pepper

*The classic method of cooking trout in butter with
flaked almonds remains a favourite with everyone.*

Coat the trout with the flour. Heat ¼ inch
(5 mm) depth of oil in a large, heavy frying pan
until very hot. Add the trout and cook over a
high heat, turning once, for about 4 minutes on
each side. Remove the fish to a heated serving
dish and keep warm. Pour off all but about 2
tablespoons (2 × 15 ml spoon) of the oil from the
pan, add the butter and stir until melted. Add the
almonds and cook over a low heat until they are
golden brown. Add the lemon juice, season if
necessary, pour the sauce over the fish and serve
at once. New potatoes and french, runner or
broad beans go well with this dish.

Baked Trout with Bacon
Trout with Almonds

BAKED TROUT WITH BACON

4 thin rashers of streaky
bacon

1 small onion, peeled and
chopped finely

4 trout, approx. 8 oz (225 g)
each, cleaned and gutted

7 fl oz (210 ml) dry white
wine

juice of 1½ lemons

2 oz (50 g) butter, cut into
small pieces

1 tablespoon (15 ml spoon)
finely chopped parsley

4 tablespoons (4 × 15 ml
spoon) fresh white
breadcrumbs

salt and freshly ground black
pepper

Oven temperature:
Gas Mark 6/400°F/200°C

*An excellent way to cook trout, with the bacon adding
an evocative flavour to the delicacy of the fish.*

Preheat the oven. Remove the bacon rinds and
cut the bacon into very thin strips. Arrange the
onion in the bottom of a lightly greased baking
dish. Season the trout lightly with salt and
pepper inside and out and lay them on the onion.
Cover the trout with the bacon, pour over the
wine and bake in the oven for 10 minutes.
Gently remove the bacon, transfer the trout to a
serving dish and keep warm.

Combine the cooking juices, onion and bacon
in a saucepan with the lemon juice, bring to the
boil and cook over a high heat, stirring, until the
sauce is reduced by about a third. Gradually beat
in the butter, stirring continuously, over a
medium heat. Add the parsley, pour the sauce
over the trout and sprinkle the breadcrumbs
over. Brown quickly under a hot grill before
serving.

FILLETS OF MACKEREL WITH A
MEDITERRANEAN TOPPING

3 large, ripe tomatoes

3 tablespoons (3 × 15 ml
spoon) olive or sunflower oil

1 onion, peeled and chopped
finely

1 clove of garlic, peeled and
crushed

1 medium-size aubergine,
cut into small dice

a pinch of dried oregano

4 mackerel, filleted

*Instead of mackerel fillets you can use whiting,
haddock or cod fillets.*

Cover the tomatoes with boiling water for 2
minutes, slide off the skin, discard the core and
seeds and chop the flesh.

Heat 2 tablespoons (2 × 15 ml spoon) of the oil
in a saucepan, add the onion and garlic and cook
over a low heat, stirring to prevent sticking,
until the onion is soft and transparent. Add the
aubergine and cook, stirring, for a further 5
minutes. Add the tomatoes, season with salt and
pepper, mix in the oregano, bring to the boil and

2 oz (50 g) butter

1 teaspoon (5 ml spoon) lemon juice

2 oz (50 g) grated Gruyère or Cheddar cheese

salt and freshly ground black pepper

simmer for 20 minutes until the vegetables are soft.

Season the mackerel fillets with salt and pepper. Heat the butter with the remaining oil in a frying pan, add the mackerel (skin side down) and cook over a medium heat for 6 minutes. Remove the fish with a spatula to a shallow baking dish. Mix the juice from the pan and the lemon juice with the vegetable mixture; spoon the mixture over the fish. Top with the cheese and brown under a medium–hot grill until the fish is hot and cooked through and the cheese topping is golden brown.

Serve with mashed potatoes or Savoury Rice (page 44) and a green vegetable.

BARBECUED MULLET

Serves 4

4 red mullet, grey mullet, mackerel or small sea bass, approx. 1 lb (450 g) each, gutted and cleaned with the heads on

8 tablespoons (8 × 15 ml spoon) sunflower oil

1½ tablespoons (4 × 5 ml spoon) dried oregano

juice of 2 lemons

coarse salt and freshly ground black pepper

To garnish:

2 tablespoons (2 × 15 ml spoon) finely chopped parsley

Dry the fish with kitchen towelling and season with salt and freshly ground black pepper inside and outside. Brush the fish with some of the oil, sprinkle with half the oregano and grill over a high heat; turn frequently, sprinkling the remaining oregano over the other side, and brushing them as they cook with the lemon juice and the remaining oil, until the skin of the fish is crisp and slightly blackened and the fish is cooked through. Transfer them to a serving dish and sprinkle over the chopped parsley.

SAVOURY RICE

8 oz (225 g) long grain rice

½ red pepper

2 tablespoons (2 × 15 ml spoon) sunflower oil

1 onion, peeled and chopped finely

1 clove of garlic, chopped finely

1 egg, beaten

2 teaspoons (2 × 5 ml spoon) soy sauce

salt and freshly ground black pepper

This is a good accompaniment for many fish dishes in place of potatoes.

Wash and drain the rice, place it in a saucepan and add enough cold water to come ¾ inch (2 cm) above the level of the rice. Season with salt and bring slowly to the boil, stirring well, cover tightly and simmer on a low heat for 20 minutes. Whip the rice with a fork to get air into it, cover tightly again and leave on the side of the stove for 10 minutes, by which time all the moisture should have been absorbed and the rice should be tender and fluffy.

Remove the core and seeds from the pepper and finely chop the flesh. Heat the oil in a frying pan, add the onion and garlic and cook over a low heat, stirring to prevent sticking, until the onion is soft and transparent. Add the pepper and cook over a medium heat for 5 minutes until the onion is golden brown and the pepper is soft. Add the rice, season with salt and pepper and stir over a high heat for 3–4 minutes. Stir in the beaten egg and the soy sauce and stir over a high heat until the egg is distributed throughout the rice and is lightly cooked.

Savoury Rice
Salmon Steaks with Courgettes and Cream
Fish Steaks with Peppercorn Sauce

SALMON STEAKS WITH COURGETTES AND CREAM

6 small courgettes

6 salmon steaks

2 oz (50 g) butter

6 bay leaves

juice of ½ lemon

2 tablespoons (2 × 15 ml spoon) dry vermouth

½ pint (300 ml) double cream

salt and freshly ground black pepper

To garnish:

1 tablespoon (15 ml spoon) finely chopped parsley

Oven temperature:
Gas Mark 5/375°F/190°C

Salmon and courgettes are both at their best (and cheapest!) in midsummer. Their flavours go well together and cooking the salmon with the courgettes ensures the fish does not dry out during the cooking time.

Cut the courgettes into small dice, place them in a colander or sieve and leave for 30 minutes. Then shake off excess water and pat the courgettes dry on kitchen paper.

Preheat the oven. Arrange the salmon steaks in a well-buttered baking dish and top each steak with the remaining butter cut into small pieces. Surround the steaks with the diced courgettes (the dish should be only just big enough to take the steaks and the courgettes), add the bay leaves and pour over the lemon juice, vermouth and cream. Season with salt and pepper, cover tightly with foil and bake in the oven for 30 minutes or until the salmon flesh is just opaque around the bone.

Remove the steaks with a slotted spoon, strip off the skin and arrange on a heated serving dish, pour over the cream and courgettes, sprinkle with the parsley and serve at once with new potatoes and crisp french beans.

FISH STEAKS WITH PEPPERCORN SAUCE

3 firm, ripe tomatoes

1½ teaspoons (3 × 2.5 ml spoon) green peppercorns, drained and rinsed

6 white fish steaks or cutlets (try hake, halibut, cod or haddock)

plain flour

2 oz (50 g) butter

¼ pint (150 ml) red wine

¼ pint (150 ml) good chicken stock (or use water and ½ stock cube)

¼ pint (150 ml) double cream

salt and freshly ground black pepper

A lovely robust dish with a delicious flavour. The dish can also be made from mackerel fillets.

Cover the tomatoes with boiling water, leave to stand for 1 minute and then slide off the skins; remove the core and seeds and chop the flesh. Mash the peppercorns with a fork. Coat the fish with flour seasoned with salt and pepper.

Heat the butter in a frying pan. Add the fish and cook over a medium-high heat for about 6 minutes on each side until just tender. Remove the fish with a slotted spoon to a heated serving dish and keep warm.

Add the wine to the juices in the pan, scraping the pan well so that all the sediment is incorporated in the sauce. Raise the heat and stir until the wine has reduced to about 3 tablespoons (3 × 15 ml spoon). Add the stock, stir well and boil until reduced to half the quantity. Add the cream and stir over a low heat until the sauce is thick and smooth. Add the tomatoes, season with a little more salt and mix in the peppercorns. Bring to the boil and pour over the fish. Serve at once with boiled or mashed potatoes and a green vegetable.

LOBSTER THERMIDOR

2 medium-size (2–2¼ lb/ 900 g–1 kg) cooked lobsters

3 oz (75 g) butter

1 small onion, peeled and chopped finely

2 tablespoons (2 × 15 ml spoon) plain flour

½ pint (300 ml) milk

1 teaspoon (5 ml spoon) made English mustard

1 tablespoon (15 ml spoon) tomato purée

a few drops each of Worcestershire and Tabasco sauces

1 egg yolk, beaten

¼ pint (150 ml) double cream

2 tablespoons (2 × 15 ml spoon) medium-dry sherry

4 tablespoons (4 × 15 ml spoon) grated parmesan cheese

3 tablespoons (3 × 15 ml spoon) dry breadcrumbs

salt and freshly ground black pepper

Crack the lobster claws and legs and remove all the meat. Split the lobster down the centre, discard any black vein and the brain sac and remove the meat from the body, reserving the shells. Cut the meat into ¾ inch (2 cm) thick slices.

Melt 2 oz (50 g) of the butter in a saucepan, add the onion and cook over a low heat until soft and transparent. Add the flour and mix well. Gradually add the milk, stirring continuously over a medium–high heat until the sauce comes to the boil and is thick and smooth. Season the sauce with salt and pepper and mix in the mustard, tomato purée and a few drops each of Worcestershire and Tabasco sauces. Beat the egg yolk with the cream until smooth, add this mixture to the sauce and stir over a low heat until the sauce is thick and glossy. Add the sherry and mix well. Add the lobster meat, mix lightly and check the seasoning.

Pile the lobster into the half-shells and top with the parmesan mixed with the breadcrumbs. Dot with the other 1 oz (25 g) butter cut into very small slivers and brown quickly under a hot grill until golden brown and bubbling.

Lobster Thermidor

MARINATED GRILLED FISH STEAKS

8 tablespoons (8 × 15 ml spoon) sunflower oil

2 cloves of garlic, crushed

1 teaspoon (5 ml spoon) mixed herbs

1½ tablespoons (4 × 5 ml spoon) lemon juice

4 fish steaks or cutlets, about 8 oz (225 g) – use either a white fish like haddock, hake or cod, or farmed salmon

butter

salt and freshly ground black pepper

To garnish:

1½ tablespoons (4 × 5 ml spoon) chopped parsley

Marinating fish steaks or cutlets before cooking the fish prevents smaller cuts of fish drying out during the cooking time.

Combine the oil, garlic, herbs and lemon juice in a screw-topped jar (or in a liquidiser or food processor), season generously with salt and pepper and shake or blend to mix. Place the fish steaks in a shallow dish just large enough to hold them, pour over the marinade and leave to stand at room temperature for 2 hours, basting with the marinade every now and then.

Generously butter a baking dish, arrange the fish in the dish, pour over the marinade and cook under a hot grill (about 4 inches/10 cm away) for 4 minutes. Baste well with the juices in the pan, turn the fish over and cook for a further 4 minutes on the other side, or until the fish is just cooked through. Transfer the fish to a heated serving dish. Sprinkle with parsley and pour over the juices from the pan. Serve at once. Buttered courgettes and boiled potatoes go well with a simple dish like this.

Note: the same marinade mixture can be used for fish that are to be baked in the oven. Arrange the fish in a well buttered baking dish, pour over the marinade and bake in a hot oven (Gas Mark 7/425°F/220°C) for about 10–12 minutes, basting every now and then with the juices in the dish.

FISH FILLETS DELAINE

1½ lb (675 g) fish fillets
(whiting, cod, haddock or
hake)

½ pint (300 ml) chicken
stock (or use water and
½ stock cube)

¼ pint (150 ml) dry white
wine

2 onions, one sliced and one
chopped finely

1 carrot, peeled and sliced

1 stick of celery, sliced

2 oz (50 g) firm button
mushrooms, sliced thinly

3 oz (75 g) butter, plus a
little extra for greasing

2 oz (50 g) fresh white
breadcrumbs

2 tablespoons (2 × 15 ml
spoon) plain flour

a pinch of chopped or dried
mixed herbs

yolks of 2 eggs

3 tablespoons (3 × 15 ml
spoon) double cream

½ oz (15 g) grated
Cheddar cheese mixed with
½ oz (15 g) grated
parmesan cheese

salt and freshly ground black
pepper

Oven temperature:
Gas Mark 5/375°F/190°C

*A rather unusual dish, in which poached fish fillets are
layered with mushrooms and crisply fried breadcrumbs
to make an interesting and savoury meal.*

Place the fish in a shallow dish, pour over the
stock and white wine, add the sliced onion,
carrot and celery and bring slowly to the boil.
Simmer for about 5 minutes until the fish is
opaque. Remove the fish with a slotted spoon
and remove any dark skin and bones. Boil the
cooking liquid until reduced by about a third and
then strain and reserve it.

Preheat the oven. Cook the mushrooms over
a high heat in ½ oz (15 g) of the butter for 2
minutes. Melt 1 oz (25 g) of the butter in a frying
pan, add three-quarters of the breadcrumbs and
cook over a high heat, stirring, until they are
crisp.

Melt a further 1½ oz (40 g) butter in a
saucepan, add the chopped onion and cook over
a low heat, stirring to prevent sticking, until the
onion is soft and transparent. Add the flour and
mix well. Gradually add ½ pint (300 ml) of the
reserved stock, stirring continuously, over a
medium–high heat until the sauce comes to the
boil and is thick and smooth. Season the sauce
with salt and freshly ground black pepper and
mix in the herbs. Beat the egg yolks with the
cream until smooth. Add the cream and egg
yolks to the sauce, stirring over a low heat until
the sauce is thick and glossy.

Arrange half the fish in a lightly buttered
shallow baking dish. Top with the mushrooms
and fried breadcrumbs and then with the
remaining fish. Pour over the sauce, sprinkle
over the remaining, unfried, breadcrumbs
mixed with the cheese and heat through in a
moderately hot oven for about 15 minutes until
the dish is bubbling and the top is golden brown.
Serve with mashed or new potatoes and a green
vegetable.

FISH, MUSHROOM AND LEEK PIE

Basic stock: Fish stock, page 6

1 lb (450 g) firm white fish (such as haddock or coley)
2 teaspoons (2 × 5 ml spoon) lemon juice
2½ oz (65 g) butter
3 small leeks, cleaned and sliced thickly
4 oz (100 g) firm button mushrooms, sliced
1½ tablespoons (4 × 5 ml spoon) plain flour
¼ pint (150 ml) fish stock or chicken stock (or water and ½ stock cube)
¼ pint (150 ml) milk
a pinch of herbs
1½ lb (675 g) potatoes, boiled and mashed with a little butter and milk
1½ oz (40 g) grated Cheddar cheese
salt and freshly ground black pepper
Oven temperature: *Gas Mark 5/375°F/190°C*

Season the fish with salt and pepper and sprinkle over the lemon juice. Steam the fish in a lightly buttered colander or steamer placed over a pan of boiling water for about 6 minutes until tender. Remove any skin and bones and flake the flesh.

Melt ½ oz (15 g) of the butter in a frying pan, add the sliced leek and cook over a low heat, stirring to prevent sticking, until it is soft and tender. Remove the leek, melt a further ½ oz (15 g) butter in the pan and add the sliced mushroom, tossing over a high heat for 2 minutes.

Melt the remaining butter in a saucepan, add the flour and mix well. Gradually blend in the stock and milk, stirring continuously over a medium–high heat until the sauce comes to the boil and is thick and smooth. Add the herbs, season with salt and pepper and simmer for 3 minutes. Lightly fold in the leek, mushroom and fish and transfer to a shallow baking dish. Spread the potatoes over, making a pattern on the top with the back of a fork, sprinkle with the cheese and bake in the oven for 30–35 minutes until the dish is heated through and the topping is golden brown.

Rich Pancakes with a Seafood Filling
Fish, Mushroom and Leek Pie

RICH PANCAKES WITH A SEAFOOD FILLING

Serves 6

Basic stock: Fish stock, page 6

For the pancake mixture:

4 oz (100 g) plain flour

a pinch of salt

4 fl oz (110 ml) beer

4 fl oz (110 ml) milk

2 oz (50 g) butter, melted, plus extra for frying

2 eggs

For the filling:

1½ oz (40 g) butter, plus extra for greasing

1 small onion, peeled and chopped finely

3 tablespoons (3 × 15 ml spoon) plain flour

½ pint (300 ml) milk

⅓ pint (200 ml) fish stock, or chicken stock (or use water and ½ stock cube)

yolks of 2 eggs

¼ pint (150 ml) double cream

12 oz (350 g) white fish fillets, cooked and flaked (use cod, hake, halibut or haddock)

4 oz (100 g) peeled prawns, fresh or thawed from frozen

1 tablespoon (15 ml spoon) finely chopped parsley

3 tablespoons (3 × 15 ml spoon) finely grated parmesan cheese

This is one of the best savoury pancake recipes I know. You can vary the filling by using some chopped spinach with the fish, by using smoked haddock instead of white fish or by using half crab and half white fish.

To make the pancakes, combine the flour, salt, beer, milk, melted butter and eggs and either whisk with a rotary whisk or process until smooth in a liquidiser or food processor. Cover with a cloth and leave to stand at room temperature for 1 hour.

Heat a non-stick pan over a medium–high heat and brush when hot with a thin film of melted butter. Add just enough batter to cover the bottom of the pan when it is whirled around (pour off any excess) and cook the pancake until just set. Turn the pancake over and cook until the other side is golden brown. Slide each pancake on to a plate and repeat the process until the batter is all used up – you should have about twelve pancakes.

To make the filling, heat the butter in a saucepan. Add the onion and cook over a low heat, stirring to prevent sticking, until it is soft and transparent. Add the flour and mix well. Gradually blend in the milk and stock, stirring continuously over a medium–high heat, until the sauce comes to the boil and is thick and smooth. Season with salt, pepper and the nutmeg and simmer for 3 minutes. Beat the egg yolks with 3 tablespoons (3 × 15 ml spoon) of the cream and beat into the sauce over a low heat, stirring and taking care not to boil, until the sauce is thick and glossy. Fold in the fish, prawns and parsley.

Preheat the oven. Place a layer of the filling down the centre of each pancake and roll up lightly. Place the pancakes in a lightly buttered baking dish, pour over the remaining cream,

54

a pinch each of nutmeg and cayenne pepper

salt and freshly ground black pepper

Oven temperature:
Gas Mark 5/375°F/190°C

sprinkle over the parmesan cheese and the cayenne and bake in the oven for about 15 minutes until the pancakes are heated through and the cheese is golden. Serve with a salad or green vegetable.

BAKED FISH WITH SAUCE DELPHINE

Serves 4

2 lb (900 g) flat fish fillets (lemon sole or plaice), with the black skin removed

½ pint (300 ml) dry white wine

1 large onion, peeled and chopped finely

1 oz (25 g) butter

5 tablespoons (5 × 15 ml spoon) dried breadcrumbs

½ pint (300 ml) mayonnaise

5 fl oz (150 ml) carton of natural yogurt

a pinch of paprika

salt and freshly ground black pepper

Oven temperature:
Gas Mark 5/375°F/190°C

By combining mayonnaise and yogurt for a topping in this recipe you can give your friends an unusual and exciting but simply prepared fish dish.

Place the fish in a shallow china dish, pour over the wine, season with salt and pepper and leave to marinate for 4 hours, spooning the wine over the fish every now and then.

Drain the marinade from the fish into a saucepan. Bring to the boil, add the onion and bring back to the boil; boil for about 15 minutes until the onion is tender. Drain well.

Preheat the oven. Arrange the fish in a buttered baking dish, sprinkle over half the breadcrumbs and dot with the remaining butter in small pieces. Combine the mayonnaise and the yogurt, season with salt and pepper, add the onion and a pinch of paprika and mix well. Spoon the sauce over the fish, sprinkle with the remaining crumbs and bake in the oven for 20 minutes or until the fish is just tender. Serve with mashed or new potatoes and green vegetables.

CRISPLY GRILLED SEA BASS

3–3½ lb (1.3–1.6 kg) sea bass

1 orange

2 sprigs of dill or parsley

1 tablespoon (15 ml spoon) lemon juice

1-inch (2.5 cm) piece of fresh root ginger

2 tablespoons (2 × 15 ml spoon) soy sauce

4 tablespoons (4 × 15 ml spoon) sunflower oil

salt and freshly ground black pepper

To garnish:

lemon wedges

To my mind sea bass are one of the finest of all our fish, being both of an exquisite flavour and an excellent moist texture. They are extremely versatile fish but are at their best when lightly stuffed, spiced and quickly grilled so that their delicious skin becomes crisp and aromatic, while the flesh remains tender and succulent. Ask your fishmonger to bone and gut the fish from the back or do this yourself, as below.

If preparing the fish yourself, cut off the fins of the fish with kitchen scissors. Using a medium, sharp-pointed knife, make an incision behind the head to one side of the backbone. Slide the knife along the backbone down the length of the fish. Do the same thing on the other side, thus releasing the backbone. Using kitchen scissors again, sever the backbone from behind the head and in front of the tail and remove the bones. Gut and clean the fish, from the other side.

Remove the peel and pith from the orange with a sharp knife and cut the flesh into slices. Season the inside of the fish with salt and pepper and stuff it on both sides with the orange, dill or parsley and half the lemon juice. Score the skin of the fish in diagonal shallow cuts. Peel the ginger root, chop it roughly and squeeze it through a garlic press. Rub the slashed skin of the fish with the ginger juice, the remaining lemon juice and the soy sauce.

Heat the grill to its hottest possible heat. Line a baking tray with foil, brush it with oil, place the fish on the foil and pour the remaining oil over. Grill the fish as near as possible to the heat for 7 minutes, turn it over with two spatulas and grill on the other side for a further 4–5 minutes. Test to see whether the fish is cooked by poking it with a sharp-pointed knife to see if the flesh at the centre is opaque – but do not overcook. Serve at once with wedges of lemon and any juices from the pan poured over.

Crisply Grilled Sea Bass

SPRATS WITH PERNOD-FLAVOURED BATTER

5 oz (150 g) plain flour

1 teaspoon (5 ml spoon)
baking powder

a pinch of cayenne pepper

¼ teaspoon (1.25 ml
spoon) dried oregano

1 bay leaf, chopped very
finely, or a pinch of ground
bay leaf

1 egg, beaten

2 teaspoons (2 × 5 ml
spoon) Pernod

¼ pint (150 ml) water

2 lb (900 g) sprats, gutted
and filleted with the heads
removed

oil for deep frying

salt and freshly ground black
pepper

To garnish:

sprigs of parsley and lemon
wedges

Combine the flour with the baking powder and mix well. Season with salt, pepper and cayenne. Add the oregano, bay leaf, egg, Pernod and water and whisk with a rotary whisk (or blend in a liquidiser or food processor) until smooth. Leave to stand for 15 minutes.

Dip the fish in the batter and fry them a handful at a time, in very hot, deep oil until golden. Drain with a slotted spoon and then on kitchen towelling and continue to fry batches of the sprats. When all the sprats are golden, reheat the oil and fry the sprats for a second time until they are crisp and golden brown. Drain again with a slotted spoon and then on kitchen towelling and keep hot until ready to serve. Fry the parsley in the hot oil.

Serve on a white napkin on a heated serving dish and garnish with the deep-fried sprigs of parsley and wedges of lemon.

SOUFFLÉ OF CHEESE AND LEMON SOLE

Serves 4

2½ oz (65 g) butter, plus extra for greasing

4 fillets of lemon sole (or plaice) with the black skin removed – approx. 1¼ lb (550 g) total weight

1½ oz (40 g) plain flour

a scant ½ pint (300 ml) milk

3 oz (75 g) cream cheese

2 oz (50 g) Cheddar cheese, grated

a pinch each of cayenne pepper and ground nutmeg

3 eggs, separated

1 tablespoon (15 ml spoon) fine dry breadcrumbs

salt and freshly ground black pepper

Oven temperature:
Gas Mark 6/400°F/200°C

As with all soufflés, the guests should wait for the dish rather than the other way round. A light dusting of breadcrumbs over the top of the soufflé will help to prevent it sinking as it comes from the oven to the table.

Butter a 2¾-pint (1.5–1.6-litre) soufflé dish generously with the extra butter. Cut each fillet in half lengthways and then cut each strip across in half.

Melt the 2½ oz (65 g) butter in a saucepan, add the flour and mix well until a ball is formed. *Gradually* beat in the milk over a high heat, beating continuously with a wooden spoon until the sauce comes to the boil and is thick and smooth. Lower the heat, add the cream cheese and mix until smooth again. Add the Cheddar cheese and season with salt, pepper, and the cayenne and nutmeg. Mix well and simmer for 2 minutes; then remove from the heat.

Preheat the oven. Beat the egg yolks until smooth and then beat them into the soufflé base in the pan. Beat the egg whites until stiff and lightly fold them into the soufflé base, using a wire whisk. Spoon a third of the soufflé mixture into the soufflé dish, arrange half the fish on the mixture and then repeat, finishing with the remaining third of the soufflé mixture on the top. Sprinkle over the breadcrumbs and bake in the oven for 25–30 minutes until the soufflé is risen and golden brown on top. Serve at once.

STEAMING FISH ON AROMATIC VEGETABLES

Serves 6

4 carrots

2 sticks of celery

1 bulb fennel (optional)

1½ oz (40 g) butter

1 tablespoon (15 ml spoon) sunflower oil

1 onion, sliced thinly into rings

¼ pint (150 ml) dry white wine

¼ pint (150 ml) chicken stock (or use water and ½ stock cube)

½ teaspoon (2.5 ml spoon) fines herbes

2 lb (900 g) centre cut halibut or turbot, on the bone

¼ pint (150 ml) single cream

salt and freshly ground black pepper

To garnish:

chopped parsley

When you have a piece of really good-quality fish one of the best and most sympathetic ways to deal with it is to steam it gently over a bed of aromatic vegetables cooked in wine. The fish remains moist and deliciously tender, losing none of its flavour and texture. Fines herbes, used in this recipe, are a classic combination of finely chopped fresh or dried herbs – usually parsley, chervil and chives, though dill or fennel may be substituted for any unavailable.

Peel the carrots and cut them into 1½-inch (4 cm) long pieces; very thinly slice them lengthways and then cut the slices into very thin sticks. Cut the celery and fennel, if used, into similar matchstick pieces.

Heat the butter with the oil in a shallow saucepan large enough to accommodate the fish. Add the onion and cook over a low heat, stirring, until it is soft and transparent. Add the carrots and celery and stir for 2 minutes. Add the wine, bring to the boil and boil over a high heat for 3 minutes to reduce; then add the stock and herbs and season with salt and pepper. Place the fish on top of the vegetables, cover tightly and steam over a very low heat for about 20 minutes until the fish is just opaque and the flesh eases away if you slide a knife along the bone. The cooking time will depend on the thickness of the fish but be careful not to overcook.

Remove the fish. Remove the vegetables with a slotted spoon to a serving dish and place the fish on top. Add the cream to the juices in the pan and heat through, to just below boiling point. Pour the sauce over the fish, sprinkle over some parsley and serve at once with boiled potatoes and green vegetables.

Steaming Fish on Aromatic Vegetables

A SUMMER FISH DISH

1½ lb (675 g) firm white
fish fillets (cod, haddock,
hake or coley), skin
removed

4 thin rashers of streaky
bacon, rinds removed

1½ oz (40 g) butter, plus
extra for greasing

4 small or 2 large courgettes

1 teaspoon (5 ml spoon)
finely chopped fresh
tarragon or ½ teaspoon (2.5
ml spoon) dried tarragon

¼ pint (150 ml) single
cream

4 tablespoons (4 × 15 ml
spoon) dry vermouth

salt and freshly ground black
pepper

Oven temperatures:
Gas Mark 8/450°F/230°C
Gas Mark 2/300°F/150°C

*A delicate and subtly flavoured dish which combines
white fish with summer courgettes, tarragon, cream
and dry vermouth. Serve it with grilled, halved
tomatoes, crisply cooked green beans and new potatoes
boiled in their skins.*

Preheat the oven to the higher temperature.
Divide the fillets into four pieces. Season the fish
with salt and pepper and wrap each piece in a
bacon rasher. Place the wrapped pieces in a
lightly buttered baking dish. Cut the courgettes
into ¾-inch (2 cm) cubes and surround the fish
with them. Cut the 1½ oz (40 g) butter into
small pieces and dot over the fish and vegetables.
Sprinkle over the tarragon and pour over the
cream mixed with the vermouth.

Cover the dish tightly with foil and bake in the
hot oven for 10 minutes; then turn the heat to the
lower setting and continue to cook for a further
20 minutes until the fish is just tender.

Note: fish cutlets, especially salmon cutlets,
also respond well to being cooked in this way.

FISH PLAKI

Serves 6

14 oz (397 g) can of
tomatoes

4 tablespoons (4 × 15 ml
spoon) finely chopped
parsley

1 clove of garlic, peeled and
crushed

2 tablespoons (2 × 15 ml
spoon) lemon juice

2 oz (50 g) fresh white
breadcrumbs

2 lb (900 g) firm white fish
fillets (e.g., cod, haddock or
hake), with the black skin
removed

4 tablespoons (4 × 15 ml
spoon) olive or sunflower oil

4 thin slices of lemon,
halved

salt and freshly ground black
pepper

a pinch of cayenne pepper

Oven temperature:
Gas Mark 4/350°F/180°C

Throughout the Mediterranean you will find a wide
variety of fish dishes which involve baking the fish in a
savoury tomato sauce. This is a typical dish from
Greece.

Preheat the oven. Combine the tomatoes,
parsley, garlic and lemon juice, season with salt,
pepper and the cayenne, bring to the boil and stir
in the breadcrumbs. Boil over a high heat for
1 minute.

Place the fish fillets in an oiled baking dish,
brush with the oil and pour over the tomato
sauce. Top with the half-slices of lemon and
bake in the oven for 40 minutes. This dish goes
well with Savoury Rice (page 44).

63

COQUILLES ST JACQUES WITH PASTRY CRESCENTS

Serves 4–6

8 medium-size scallops

½ pint (300 ml) dry white wine

1 small onion, peeled and chopped finely

bouquet garni

2 oz (50 g) firm button mushrooms, sliced thinly

juice of ½ lemon

2½ oz (65 g) butter

1 medium-size onion, peeled and chopped

2 tablespoons (2 × 15 ml spoon) plain flour

1 small egg, beaten, plus an extra yolk

4 tablespoons (4 × 15 ml spoon) double cream

7½ oz (225 g) packet of frozen puff pastry, thawed

salt and freshly ground black pepper

Oven temperature:
Gas Mark 6/400°F/200°C

Coquilles St Jacques with Pastry Crescents ▶

The flavour of scallops is so delicate that it is a crime to cook them in any but the most simple ways. One of my favourites is merely to slice them, add them to some onions and small pieces of bacon softened in butter, season the dish with salt and pepper, add 1 tablespoon (15 ml spoon) finely chopped fresh sage and 2 tablespoons (2 × 15 ml spoon) dry white wine and cook for 3 minutes only. Another delightful way of serving scallops is this classic but simple recipe.

Remove any black veins from the scallops. Place the scallops in a saucepan with the white wine, the small onion and the bouquet garni, add just enough water to cover the scallops and season with salt and pepper. Bring very gently to the boil and simmer for 3 minutes. Drain the scallops, boil the cooking liquid until reduced by a third, strain and reserve. Separate the corals from the scallops and cut each scallop into three slices. Blanch the mushrooms in boiling, salted water, to which the lemon juice has been added, for 2 minutes and drain well.

Melt 2 oz (50 g) of the butter in a clean pan, add the other onion and cook over a low heat until it is soft and transparent. Add the flour and mix well. Gradually add the reserved cooking liquid, stirring continuously over a medium-high heat until the sauce comes to the boil and is thick and smooth. Beat the egg yolk with the cream and whisk it into the sauce, stirring, without boiling, until the sauce is rich and glossy. Season with salt and pepper. Add the mushrooms and the scallops to the sauce and divide the mixture between 4–6 scallop shells or shallow dishes. Dot with the remaining ½ oz (15 g) butter cut into small pieces.

Preheat the oven. Roll out the thawed pastry to about one-eighth inch (3 mm) thickness and cut into small crescent shapes. Score the top of

the crescents with a criss-cross pattern and brush with beaten egg, place them on a baking sheet and bake in the oven for about 5 minutes until they are well risen and golden brown.

Reheat the scallops under a hot grill until bubbling and golden and garnish with some of the pastry crescents, serving the rest as an accompaniment.

GRILLED FISH WITH CELERY SAUCE

Serves 4

6 sticks of celery

3 oz (75 g) butter

1 small onion, peeled and chopped finely

5 teaspoons (5 × 5 ml spoon) plain flour

a scant ½ pint (300 ml) milk

a pinch of ground nutmeg

4 large or 8 small fillets of lemon sole or plaice, with the dark skin removed

salt and freshly ground black pepper

The secret of this dish is to cut the celery into really thin julienne strips and to use the inner, more tender, celery stalks.

Trim off the leaves of the celery, chop them finely and put on one side. Cut the celery stalks lengthways into 1½-inch (4 cm) long, thin matchstick strips. Blanch in boiling water for 2 minutes and drain well.

Melt 2 oz (50 g) of the butter in a saucepan, add the onion and celery and cook over a low heat, stirring to prevent sticking, until the vegetables are really soft. Add the flour and mix well. Gradually blend in the milk over a medium-high heat, stirring continuously, until the sauce comes to the boil and is thick and smooth. Season the sauce with salt, pepper and nutmeg and simmer for 5 minutes.

Place the fish on a foil-covered, lightly buttered, grill pan and season with salt and pepper. Melt the remaining butter and brush over the fish. Grill under a medium-high heat for about 5–7 minutes until the fish is just cooked. Arrange on a serving dish, pour over the sauce and garnish with the reserved chopped celery leaves. Grilled tomato halves and broccoli are good accompaniments to this dish.

MOUSSAKA OF VEGETABLES AND MACKEREL

3 medium-size mackerel, cleaned and gutted

1 small onion, peeled and sliced

1 small carrot, peeled and sliced

a bouquet garni

1 chicken stock cube

2 tablespoons (2 × 15 ml spoon) sunflower oil

2 large onions, peeled and chopped finely

12 oz (350 g) aubergines, cut into small dice

15 oz (425 g) can of tomatoes

½ pint (300 ml) red wine

a pinch of dried oregano

4 bay leaves

2 eggs

¼ pint (150 ml) milk

2 oz (50 g) grated Cheddar cheese

a pinch of ground nutmeg

salt and freshly ground black pepper

Oven temperature:
Gas Mark 4/350°F/180°C

A fish version of lamb moussaka which makes a well-flavoured, interesting and unusual dish.

Place the fish in a shallow pan; add the sliced small onion and carrot and enough water to cover the fish. Add the bouquet garni, season with salt and pepper and sprinkle over the crumbled stock cube. Bring gently to the boil, cover and poach the fish gently for about 8 minutes, until just tender. Remove the fish with a slotted spoon and boil the liquid over a high heat until it is reduced to about ¼ pint (150 ml). Strain the liquid and reserve it.

Heat the oil in a saucepan and add the chopped large onions. Cook over a low heat, stirring to prevent sticking, until they are soft and transparent. Add the aubergines and cook over a medium heat until the oil has been absorbed. Add the tomatoes, red wine and the reserved cooking liquid, season with salt and pepper and mix in the oregano and bay leaves. Stir well and cook, uncovered, for about 20 minutes over a high heat until the aubergine is tender, the mixture is thick and most of the liquid has been absorbed. Remove the bay leaves. Preheat the oven.

Remove the skin and bones from the mackerel. Place half the vegetable mixture in a shallow baking dish. Place the fish on top of the mixture and cover with the remaining vegetable mixture.

Beat the eggs with the milk until smooth. Add the cheese and season with salt, pepper and the nutmeg. Pour the egg and milk mixture over the fish and vegetables and bake for 30–40 minutes, until the topping is set firm. Serve with rice and a green vegetable.

BAKED FISH VILLA HANBURY

Serves 6

3 × 1–1½ lb (450–675 g) grey mullet, sea bass or large mackerel, gutted and with the scales removed

4 tablespoons (4 × 15 ml spoon) olive or sunflower oil

2 teaspoons (2 × 5 ml spoon) finely chopped fresh sage leaves

2 cloves of garlic, crushed

1-inch (2.5 cm) piece of fresh root ginger, minced

2 teaspoons (2 × 5 ml spoon) lemon juice

2 thin rashers of streaky bacon, rinds removed

3 large tomatoes

salt and freshly ground black pepper

Oven temperature:
Gas Mark 5/375°F/190°C

Slash each fish in three diagonal cuts on each side. Place the fish in a shallow baking dish and pour over the oil mixed with the sage, garlic, ginger, lemon juice and salt and pepper. Leave in a cool place to marinate, basting occasionally, for 1 hour.

Preheat the oven. Mince the bacon. Cover the tomatoes with boiling water, leave them to stand for 30 seconds and then slide off the skins; remove the cores and seeds and chop the flesh roughly. Press a little bacon into each slash in the fish, cover the fish with the tomatoes and spoon over the marinade.

Bake in the oven for about 30 minutes, until a sharp-pointed knife plunged through to the backbone shows the flesh is just opaque throughout. Arrange the fish on a heated serving dish. Transfer the tomatoes and the juices in the dish to a small saucepan, bring to the boil and boil hard for 5 minutes to reduce the sauce. Pour the sauce over the fish and serve at once.

Baked Fish Villa Hanbury

STIR-FRIED CRAB WITH SWEET AND SOUR SAUCE

Serves 4–6

2 medium-size crabs, cooked

1-inch (2.5 cm) piece of fresh root ginger

2 cloves of garlic

1 small chilli pepper

6 spring onions

1 tablespoon (15 ml spoon) cornflour

4 tablespoons (4 × 15 ml spoon) soy sauce

4 tablespoons (4 × 15 ml spoon) white wine vinegar

2 tablespoons (2 × 15 ml spoon) brown sugar

¼ pint (150 ml) chicken stock

3 tablespoons (3 × 15 ml spoon) oil

Clean the crabs with a damp cloth and remove the claws and legs. Break the claws with a hammer wrapped in a cloth and remove all the meat from the claws and legs. Remove the shells, discard the stomach sacs from behind the eyes and cut each shell in half across the centre. Discard the feathery fingers from the crab bodies and cut each body into four, using a sharp knife.

Peel and very finely chop the ginger and garlic. Remove the seeds from the chilli pepper (wash your hands immediately after doing this) and chop the flesh finely. Trim the spring onions and cut them lengthways. Combine the cornflour, soy sauce, vinegar, brown sugar and stock and mix well.

Heat the oil in a large wok or a large, heavy frying pan. Add the garlic, ginger and chilli and cook over a high heat, stirring, for 30 seconds. Add the spring onions and stir for another 30 seconds. Add the crab meat, claws, legs, bodies and shells and stir over a high heat for 2 minutes. Pour over the sauce ingredients and stir over a high heat for about 2 minutes until the sauce is shining, the ingredients are lightly coated with the sauce and the crab is hot through. Transfer to a serving dish and serve with rice.

The only way to eat crab cooked like this is with the fingers. Provide nutcrackers and small forks for picking the crab from the body and claws and have fingerbowls and plenty of paper napkins on the table.

A TOUCH OF SPRING

Serves 6

1½ lb (675 g) firm white
fish fillets (cod, pollock,
whiting, haddock or hake),
skinned

1 teaspoon (5 ml spoon)
lemon juice

2 lb (900 g) potatoes, peeled

2 tablespoons (2 × 15 ml
spoon) single cream

3½ oz (90 g) butter

3 medium-size onions,
peeled and chopped roughly

8 oz (225 g) shelled green
peas

3 tablespoons (3 × 15 ml
spoon) sunflower oil

1½ tablespoons (4 × 5 ml
spoon) plain flour

½ pint (300 ml) milk

3 oz (75 g) grated Cheddar
cheese

1 egg

salt, freshly ground black
pepper, and a pinch each of
ground nutmeg and cayenne
pepper

Oven temperature:
Gas Mark 6/400°F/200°C

*Fresh garden peas (or you can use frozen) with a
topping of lightly cooked fish, a border of mashed
potatoes and the golden yellow of a cheese sauce make
this a colourful spring or summer dish.*

Cut the fish into ¾-inch (2 cm) wide strips,
sprinkle with the lemon juice, season with salt
and pepper and leave to stand for 20 minutes.

Cook the potatoes in salt water until soft.
Drain well and mash them until smooth and
fluffy with the cream, ½ oz (15 g) of the butter
and a little salt and pepper.

Melt another 1½ oz (40g) butter in a
saucepan, add the onions and cook over a low
heat until soft. Add the peas and cook over a
medium heat until they are tender. Purée the
peas in a liquidiser or food processor and season
them with salt and pepper.

Pat the fish fillets dry with kitchen paper. Heat
the oil in a frying pan, add the fish and cook for
about 3 minutes on each side until the flesh is
opaque. Drain on kitchen paper towelling.
Preheat the oven.

Heat the remaining butter in a saucepan, add
the flour and mix well. Gradually beat in the
milk, stirring continually over a medium–high
heat until the sauce comes to the boil and is thick
and smooth. Add 2 oz (50 g) of the cheese,
season with salt, pepper, cayenne and nutmeg
and stir over a low heat until the cheese has
melted. Add the egg and beat until smooth.
Remove from the heat.

Make a ring of potatoes around an oval
ovenproof serving dish. Spread the pea purée in
the centre, place the fish over the peas and pour
the sauce over the fish. Sprinkle over the
remaining cheese and heat in the oven until the
fish and vegetables are thoroughly hot and the
cheese sauce is golden and bubbling.

71

SUPPER DISHES

Garlic-stuffed Mussels
Grilled Fish with Cheese
and Tomatoes
Friday Fish Pie

GARLIC-STUFFED MUSSELS

Serves 6

3 lb (1.3 kg) mussels

¼ pint (150 ml) dry white wine

3 cloves of garlic, peeled and crushed

4 teaspoons (4 × 5 ml spoon) olive or sunflower oil

4 oz (100 g) butter

4 tablespoons (4 × 15 ml spoon) very finely chopped parsley

4 teaspoons (4 × 5 ml spoon) very finely chopped chives

4 cream cracker biscuits

salt and freshly ground black pepper

A wonderful way of serving mussels for those who like garlic; the stuffing is similar to that used for snails.

Scrub the mussels under cold running water and remove any barnacles with a knife. Pull out the wiry beards from the sides of the shells. Place the mussels in a large, heavy pan and cook, covered, over a high heat, shaking the pan every now and then, for about 6 minutes until all the mussels have opened (discard any that don't). Remove from the heat and leave until cool enough to handle.

Remove the mussels from the shells, reserving half the shells. Place the mussels in a saucepan with the wine, season with salt and freshly ground black pepper, simmer for 3 minutes for the mussels to absorb the flavour of the wine, and then drain.

Beat the garlic with the oil and butter until smooth. Season with salt and pepper and mix in the parsley and chives. Crush the cream crackers with a rolling pin into fine crumbs. Place a mussel on each half shell and, using a small knife, spread over some garlic butter. Sprinkle each mussel with a little of the cracker crumbs and grill them quickly under a high heat until the butter has melted and is bubbling. Serve with french bread.

Note: mussels cooked in the same way can also be served cold on the half shell, masked with some mayonnaise flavoured with a little lemon juice and Dijon mustard, to make an excellent first course.

FRIDAY FISH PIE

1 lb (450 g) firm white fish fillets (use cod, haddock or coley)

2½ oz (65 g) butter, plus extra for greasing

2 tablespoons (2 × 15 ml spoon) plain flour

¼ pint (150 ml) milk

4 oz (100 g) frozen peas

a pinch of ground nutmeg

2 oz (50 g) peeled prawns, fresh or thawed from frozen

3 hard-boiled eggs, shelled and sliced

3 tablespoons (3 × 15 ml spoon) milk or single cream

1½ lb (675 g) potatoes, peeled, boiled and mashed

salt and freshly ground black pepper

Oven temperature:
Gas Mark 4/350°F/180°C

You don't have to eat this on a Friday: it's good any day of the week.

Place the fish in a buttered baking dish, season with salt and pepper, dot with ½ oz (15 g) of the butter, cover with foil and bake in the oven for 20 minutes or until the fish is just tender. Drain off and reserve any cooking juices. Remove any skin from the fish and flake the flesh. Leave the oven on.

Melt a further 1½ oz (40 g) butter in a saucepan, add the flour and mix well. Gradually blend in the ¼ pint (150 ml) milk and ¼ pint (150 ml) of the cooking juices, stirring continuously over a medium-high heat until the sauce comes to the boil and is thick and smooth. Add the peas and cook over a low heat until tender. Season the sauce with salt, pepper and nutmeg and fold in the fish and prawns. Spoon half the mixture into a baking dish, top with the hard-boiled egg and cover with the remaining fish and sauce.

Beat the remaining ½ oz (15 g) butter and the remaining milk (or the cream) into the potatoes and season with salt and pepper. Spread the potato over the pie, decorate the top with a pattern made with the back of a fork and return to the oven for 30–35 minutes until the dish is hot through and the top of the mashed potato is crisp and golden.

GRILLED FISH WITH CHEESE AND TOMATOES

Serves 4

2 oz (50 g) butter

2 lb (900 g) fish fillets (use lemon sole, halibut, hake, cod, haddock or mackerel), with the dark skin removed

4 tablespoons (4 × 15 ml spoon) dry cider

2 large, ripe tomatoes, cut into very thin slices

2 oz (50 g) Cheddar cheese, cut into very thin slices

salt and freshly ground black pepper

A simple but delicious dish which takes no time at all to prepare and only a few minutes to cook.

Butter a shallow baking dish or grill pan with ½ oz (15 g) of the butter; arrange the fish in the dish and season with salt and pepper. Melt the remaining butter and pour it over the fish. Cook under a medium–hot grill for 3 minutes, turn over, baste with the juices in the pan, pour over the cider and grill for a further 3 minutes.

Baste again and then top the fish with slices of tomato and cheese. Return to the grill for about 4 minutes until the cheese has melted and is golden brown. Serve with baked potatoes and perhaps a simple green vegetable.

FAMILY FISH FRIES

Serves 4–5

1 lb (450 g) white fish fillets (e.g., whiting, cod or haddock), with the black skin removed

4 oz (100 g) streaky bacon, with the rind removed

1 egg, beaten

5 oz (150 g) self-raising flour

¼ pint (150 ml) milk

1 tablespoon (15 ml spoon) tomato purée

4 oz (100 g) drained canned sweetcorn

1 tablespoon (15 ml spoon) finely chopped parsley

oil for frying

salt and freshly ground black pepper

Cut the fish and the bacon rashers into very small dice. Whisk the egg with the flour, milk and tomato purée until a smooth batter is formed. Add the bacon, fish, sweetcorn and parsley, season with salt and pepper and mix well.

Heat some oil in a frying pan until very hot. Drop large tablespoons (15 ml spoons) of the mixture into the oil and cook over a high heat, turning once and flattening the 'fries' with a spatula, for about 3 minutes on each side until crisp and golden brown. Serve with a green vegetable and mashed or chipped potatoes.

Note: leftover chopped vegetables can be used instead of sweetcorn. You can also substitute leftover cooked fish for the raw diced fish.

STUFFED HERRINGS

4 fresh herrings

1 oz (25 g) butter, plus
extra for greasing

2 rashers of streaky bacon,
rinds removed, minced

1 small onion, peeled and
chopped

2 oz (50 g) mushrooms,
chopped finely

3 tablespoons (3 × 15 ml
spoon) fresh white
breadcrumbs

1 tablespoon (15 ml spoon)
finely chopped parsley

a small pinch of mixed herbs

2 tablespoons (2 × 15 ml
spoon) single cream

1 hard-boiled egg, chopped
finely

salt and freshly ground black
pepper

Oven temperature:
Gas Mark 5/375°F/190°C

*A simple and homely dish but one which has a good
flavour.*

Remove the backbones from the herrings,
leaving on the heads and tails. Wash and pat the
fish dry with kitchen towelling. Preheat the
oven.

Melt the 1 oz (25 g) butter in a frying pan, add
the bacon and cook over a low heat, stirring to
prevent sticking, for 3 minutes. Add the onion
and cook over a low heat until it is soft and
transparent. Add the mushroom and stir over a
medium heat for 2 minutes. Remove from the
heat, add the breadcrumbs, parsley, mixed herbs
and cream, mix well and season with salt and
pepper. Add the chopped hard-boiled egg to the
stuffing and mix well.

Spread the stuffing over the herrings, press
them firmly together and arrange in a well-
buttered baking dish. Dot with a little extra
butter, season the fish with a little extra salt and
pepper and bake in the oven for 20–25 minutes
until just cooked through. Serve with wedges of
lemon and a mustard or tomato sauce.

Note: this dish can also be made with mackerel
or with boned sprats, allowing about 5 sprats per
person.

EXCELLENT FISH CAKES

Serves 4

1 oz (25 g) butter

1 onion, peeled and chopped finely

1½ lb (675 g) potatoes, peeled and boiled

3 eggs

a pinch each of cayenne pepper and ground nutmeg

1–2 tablespoons (1–2 × 15 ml spoon) finely chopped parsley

12 oz (350 g) flaked cooked fish (use cod or any other firm white fish, or use cooked salmon for special occasions)

a little plain flour

3–4 oz (75–100 g) dried breadcrumbs

oil or lard for frying

salt and freshly ground black pepper

Melt the butter in a saucepan, add the onion and cook over a low heat, stirring to prevent sticking, until the onion is soft and transparent. Mash the potatoes until smooth and mix in the onion and the juices from the saucepan. Whisk 2 eggs until smooth and beat them into the potato mixture. Season with salt, pepper, cayenne and nutmeg and mix in the parsley. Mix in the fish and chill the mixture in a refrigerator for at least an hour.

Using floured hands, shape the mixture into eight flat, round cakes. Coat the cakes in the remaining egg, beaten, and then in dried breadcrumbs. Chill until required.

Heat ¼ inch (5 mm) oil or lard in a frying pan until smoking. Add the fish cakes and fry for about 5 minutes on each side until the cakes are crisp and a colourful golden brown.

Note: for a change try crushing sage and onion stuffing mix and using it instead of the plain breadcrumbs.

SMOKED FISH SOUFFLÉ

8 oz (225 g) smoked
haddock or smoked cod fillets

1½ oz (40 g) butter

2 tablespoons (2 × 15 ml
spoon) finely grated
parmesan cheese

1 tablespoon (15 ml spoon)
finely grated Cheddar cheese

1½ oz (40 g) plain flour

½ pint (300 ml) milk

1 tablespoon (15 ml spoon)
lemon juice

1 teaspoon (5 ml spoon)
Dijon mustard

a pinch each of ground
nutmeg and cayenne pepper

4 eggs, separated

1 tablespoon (15 ml spoon)
finely chopped parsley

1 tablespoon (15 ml spoon)
fine, fresh, white
breadcrumbs

salt and freshly ground black
pepper

Oven temperature:
Gas Mark 4/350°F/180°C

Steam the fish in a lightly buttered steamer or
colander over boiling water until the fish is just
tender (about 5–6 minutes). Remove any skin
and flake the flesh. Grease a 3-pint (1.8-litre)
soufflé dish with ½ oz (15 g) of the butter.
Sprinkle half the parmesan and all the Cheddar
around the sides of the dish. Preheat the oven.

Melt the remaining 1 oz (25 g) butter in a
saucepan, add the flour and mix well. Gradually
blend in the milk, stirring continuously over a
medium-high heat until the mixture is thick and
smooth. Add the lemon juice and mustard and
season with salt, pepper and the nutmeg and
cayenne. Remove from the heat and beat in the
egg yolks one by one, beating after each addition
until the soufflé base is smooth and shining. Fold
in the fish and parsley. Beat the egg whites until
stiff and firm and fold them lightly into the
soufflé mixture, using a large metal spoon or a
wire whisk. Sprinkle the breadcrumbs, mixed
with the remaining parmesan, over the top.

Bake the soufflé in the oven for 35 minutes or
until it has risen up over the top of the dish and
the topping is golden brown.

GRILLED MUSTARDY MACKEREL

4 mackerel, cleaned and gutted

2 tablespoons (2 × 15 ml spoon) Dijon mustard

1½ teaspoons (3 × 2.5 ml spoon) lemon juice

sunflower oil

salt and freshly ground black pepper

Mustard and the slightly oily texture of mackerel make a very successful partnership. The dish can be served with the traditional gooseberry sauce described below.

Cut five diagonal slashes on each side of the mackerel and spread the mustard in the slashes. Season the fish with salt and pepper, brush with lemon juice and oil and grill under a medium-high grill, turning once, about 6 minutes on each side – until the fish are just cooked through to the bone and the skin is crisp.

GOOSEBERRY SAUCE

12 oz (350 g) gooseberries, fresh or frozen

½ oz (15 g) butter

a pinch of ground ginger

sugar

Top and tail the gooseberries and put in a saucepan with enough water to come three-quarters of the way up them. Bring to the boil and simmer until the fruit is tender. Rub the fruit through a sieve to remove the seeds and return to a clean pan. Beat in the butter; then stir in the ginger and enough sugar to take the very sharp edge off the fruit. The sauce should be sharp but not mouth-puckering and the amount of sugar you use will depend on the tartness of the fruit.

Gooseberry Sauce
Grilled Mustardy Mackerel

FISH-STUFFED BAKED POTATOES

4 large potatoes

oil

coarse salt

10 oz (275 g) white fish fillets (e.g., cod, whiting, haddock or hake)

a little butter for greasing

4 oz (100 g) cream cheese

1 clove of garlic, peeled and crushed

1 tablespoon (15 ml spoon) finely chopped chives

salt and freshly ground black pepper

To garnish:

4 anchovies, drained

Oven temperatures:
Gas Mark 6/400°F/200°C
Gas Mark 4/350°F/180°C

Baked potatoes make a good, inexpensive supper dish. The potatoes can be baked in advance and then stuffed and reheated.

Scrub the potatoes, rub them with oil and then with coarse salt, and bake in a hot oven for 1 hour or until soft (test with a skewer to see that the potatoes are tender through to the centre). Leave to cool.

Steam the fish in a lightly buttered steamer or colander over boiling water for about 6 minutes until just tender. Remove any black skin and flake the flesh.

When the potatoes are cool, cut a slice off the top of each and scoop out the flesh into a basin. Mash with the cream cheese and garlic until smooth. Season with salt and pepper and fold in the fish and chives. Fill each potato shell with this mixture, piling it up in a dome, and top with an anchovy cut into two lengthways. Bake the filled potatoes at the lower heat until the filling is heated through and the outer skins are crisp.

SPICY-TOPPED BAKED FISH

4 medium-size tomatoes

1 aubergine

approx. 3 tablespoons (3 × 15 ml spoon) sunflower oil

1 large onion, peeled and chopped finely

2 cloves of garlic, crushed

1 teaspoon (5 ml spoon) tomato purée

1 teaspoon (5 ml spoon) dried oregano

4 fillets of white fish (whiting or any other firm-fleshed white fish)

juice of ½ lemon

2 oz (50 g) Cheddar or Gruyère cheese, grated

salt and freshly ground black pepper

A ratatouille-type topping to fillets of fish produces an aromatic and robust supper dish.

Cover the tomatoes with boiling water and leave to stand for 1 minute. Drain, slide off the skins, discard the core and seeds and roughly chop the flesh. Cut the aubergine into small dice.

Heat 2 tablespoons (2 × 15 ml spoon) oil in a saucepan. Add the onion, garlic and aubergine and cook over a low heat, stirring to prevent sticking, until the onion and aubergine are soft. Add the tomatoes, tomato purée and oregano, season with salt and freshly ground black pepper, bring to the boil and simmer gently for 20 minutes until the aubergine is absolutely soft. Purée through a sieve or in an electric liquidiser or food processor.

Heat a thin film of oil in a frying pan. Add the fish and cook over a medium heat until just tender and opaque. Arrange in a shallow baking dish and season with salt and pepper. Mix the lemon juice with any juices from the pan in which the fish was cooked.

Spread the fish with the tomato and aubergine purée, pour over the lemon and juice from the pan and top with the grated cheese. Grill under a medium–high heat until the cheese has melted and is bubbling. I would serve this sort of fish dish with Savoury Rice (page 44) and a green vegetable.

PARSLEY OMELETTE WITH CREAMED FISH

Serves 4

2 oz (50 g) firm button
mushrooms, sliced thinly

a little lemon juice

12 oz (350 g) firm white
fish fillet (e.g., cod, haddock
or coley), cooked and with
the skin removed

3½ oz (90 g) butter

1½ tablespoons (4 × 5 ml
spoon) plain flour

½ pint (300 ml) milk

1½ oz (40 g) Cheddar
cheese, grated

7 eggs

4 tablespoons (4 × 15 ml
spoon) water

2 tablespoons (2 × 15 ml
spoon) finely chopped
parsley

salt and freshly ground black
pepper

*Another quick dish which makes the centrepiece of a
good family supper.*

Blanch the mushrooms in boiling, salted water
and lemon juice for 2 minutes and drain well.
Flake the fish.

Melt 1½ oz (40 g) of the butter in a saucepan,
add the flour and mix well. Gradually blend in
the milk, stirring continuously, over a medium-
high heat until the sauce comes to the boil and is
thick and smooth. Season with salt and pepper
and mix in the cheese. Stir over a medium heat
for 2 minutes until the cheese has melted and
then fold in the mushrooms and fish. Put on one
side.

Beat the eggs lightly with the water and
season with salt and pepper. Heat half the
remaining butter in a non-stick frying pan until
foaming. Add half the beaten eggs and shake the
pan over the heat. Stir the eggs lightly with a
wooden or plastic spatula, sprinkle over half the
parsley and cook over a low heat until just set.
Place half the fish mixture along the centre of the
omelette and slide it, folding the omelette over
as you do so, on to a heated serving dish. Keep
warm while making a second omelette in the
same way.

If you have any leftover potatoes sauté those
in a little butter and oil to go with the omelettes
and serve them with a green or mixed salad.
Crisp, hot french bread goes well with this
simple dish, too.

*Traditional Kedgeree
Parsley Omelette with Creamed Fish*

TRADITIONAL KEDGEREE

12 oz (350 g) middle cut of
salmon or smoked haddock,
cooked

4 oz (100 g) butter

1 onion, peeled and chopped
finely

¼ teaspoon (1.25 ml
spoon) curry powder

6 oz (175 g) rice, cooked

2 eggs

¼ pint (150 ml) single
cream

4 hard-boiled eggs,
quartered

salt and freshly ground black
pepper

To garnish:

1 tablespoon (15 ml spoon)
finely chopped parsley

*This is a dish which has its origins in India. A little
curry powder is essential but the flavour should not be
too strong because, remember, this is traditionally a
breakfast dish. I recommend it for a summer lunch or
supper or on Sundays, if you occasionally have brunch
rather than either breakfast or lunch. The dish can be
extravagant or reasonably modest, depending on
whether you use smoked haddock or salmon as your
main ingredient – both are delicious.*

Remove any skin and bones from the fish and
flake the flesh. Heat the butter in a large, heavy
frying pan. Add the onion and cook over a low
heat, stirring to prevent sticking, until it is soft
and transparent. Add the curry powder and mix
well. Add the cooked rice and toss over a
medium heat until the rice is heated through.

Beat the eggs with the cream until smooth.
Add this mixture, with the hard-boiled eggs, to
the rice and fish. Season with salt and pepper and
stir the ingredients lightly together over a
medium heat until the beaten eggs are creamy
and the dish is heated through. Serve at once
with the parsley sprinkled over the top.

TEMPTATION

*12 oz (350 g) firm white
fish fillets (e.g., cod, hake or
whiting), with the skin
removed*

*1 can of anchovy fillets,
drained and chopped*

*2 lb (900 g) potatoes, peeled
and sliced thinly*

*2 large onions, peeled and
sliced thinly*

*¼ pint (150 ml) single
cream*

2 oz (50 g) butter, melted

*salt and freshly ground black
pepper*

Oven temperature:
Gas Mark 4/350°F/180°C

*This is a variation on a classic Swedish dish called
Jansson's Temptation, which with the addition of
fresh fish makes a delicious and hearty supper.*

Preheat the oven. Cut the fish into thin strips,
¾ inch (2 cm) long. Drain the anchovies,
reserving the oil, and chop. Arrange half the
potato slices in a well-greased baking dish about
12 × 10 × 1¾ inches (30 × 25 × 4 cm). Cover
with half the onion and top with the fish and the
chopped anchovies. Season with salt and
pepper. Cover the fish with the rest of the onion
and top with the remaining potato slices,
overlapping them neatly on top of the dish.
Season with a little more salt and pepper.

Pour over the anchovy oil and cream and
brush the potatoes with all the melted butter.
Cover with foil and bake in the oven for 1 hour,
removing the foil for the last 15–20 minutes of
cooking time so that the top layer of potatoes
becomes golden brown.

CRISP FISH IN PITTA BREAD

Serves 6

3 firm, ripe tomatoes

4 spring onions

2 tablespoons (2 × 15 ml spoon) olive or sunflower oil

2 tablespoons (2 × 15 ml spoon) white wine vinegar

½ teaspoon (2.5 ml spoon) Dijon mustard

a pinch of mixed herbs

1 lb (450 g) firm white fish fillets (e.g., cod, coley or haddock)

2 eggs, beaten

3–4 oz (75–100 g) golden breadcrumbs

oil for deep frying

3 pitta bread

salt and freshly ground black pepper

Oven temperature:
Gas Mark 6/400°F/200°C

Pitta bread makes a lovely vehicle for snack meals that are to be eaten in the fingers. Instead of a tomato salad you could use coleslaw.

Thinly slice the tomatoes, trim and slice the spring onions and arrange both together in a shallow dish. Combine the oil, vinegar and mustard and mix well. Season with salt and pepper, mix in the herbs and pour the dressing over the tomato and spring onion. Leave to stand for 10 minutes.

Preheat the oven. Cut the fish into strips 2 inches (5 cm) long and ½ inch (1 cm) thick. Dip the fish in the beaten egg and then in the breadcrumbs and deep-fry in hot oil until crisp. Drain the fish on kitchen towelling and keep warm.

Heat the pitta bread in the oven for 10 minutes. Cut each bread in half across the middle and open up the centre with a knife. Fill the bottom of the bread with the tomato salad, top with the crispy fish strips and serve at once with the bread wrapped in paper napkins.

Neapolitan Fish Pizzas
Crisp Fish in Pitta Bread
Crumpet and Fish Savouries

NEAPOLITAN FISH PIZZAS

Serves 4

4 × approx. 6 oz (175 g)
white fish steaks (haddock,
hake, whiting or coley)

4 thin rashers of streaky
bacon

3 medium-size, ripe
tomatoes

8 black olives

a pinch of oregano

2 tablespoons (2 × 15 ml
spoon) olive oil

2 oz (50 g) mozzarella or
Cheddar cheese, cut into
wafer-thin slices

salt and freshly ground black
pepper

Oven temperature:
Gas Mark 5/375°F/190°C

*These unusual slimline pizzas have a fish rather than
a dough base.*

Remove the skin from the fish steaks and season
with salt and freshly ground black pepper.
Remove the rind from the bacon and cut the
rashers into long, thin strips. Cover the
tomatoes with boiling water, leave to stand for
about 1 minute and then drain and slide off the
skins; cut the flesh into thin slices.

Preheat the oven. Arrange the fish in an oiled
baking dish. Cover the top of the fish with slices
of tomato and then with a lattice pattern of the
bacon strips. Cut the olives in slices from their
stones and dot the lattice pattern with the olive
slices. Sprinkle with a little oregano, brush with
the oil, season with pepper and cover with the
slices of cheese.

Bake in the oven for about 20 minutes until
the fish is just cooked and the cheese has melted
and is golden brown. Serve with baked potatoes
and a salad.

CRUMPET AND FISH SAVOURIES

Serves 4

4 crumpets

2 large tomatoes

1 lb (450 g) cod or haddock
fillets, with skins removed

a squeeze of lemon juice

½ oz (15 g) butter, melted

2 oz (50 g) grated Edam,
Gruyère or Emmenthal
cheese

4 anchovy fillets

*A quick snack or supper meal which tastes as good as it
looks.*

Toast the crumpets until light golden. Cut two
thick slices from the middle of each tomato (use
the remainder for garnishing, for salad or in a
stock pot). Trim the fish to the same size as the
crumpets (use the trimmings in a fish soup).

Spread each crumpet with butter and cover
with a thick slice of tomato. Place a circle of fish
on top of the tomato and brush with a little
lemon juice; season with a little salt and pepper.

salt and freshly ground black pepper

Sprinkle over the cheese and top with an anchovy. Grill under a hot grill for about 6 minutes until the cheese has melted and is bubbling and golden brown and the fish is just cooked through.

PAPRIKA FISH

2 oz (50 g) butter

1 tablespoon (15 ml spoon) sunflower oil

3 onions, peeled and sliced thinly

3 medium-size potatoes, peeled and cut into ¾-inch (2 cm) dice

1 green pepper and 1 small red pepper, with the core and seeds removed, cut into thin rings

1½ tablespoons (4 × 5 ml spoon) paprika

approx. 7 fl oz (210 ml) water

1½ lb (675 g) haddock fillet (or fillet of any firm white fish)

salt and freshly ground black pepper

A spicy, delicious dish that goes down well on a cold evening.

Heat the butter with the oil in a large, heavy frying pan. Add the onion and potato and cook over a low heat, stirring to prevent sticking, until the vegetables are golden. Add the peppers and paprika and season with salt and pepper. Mix in the water and cook over a low heat, covered, for 20 minutes until the vegetables are soft.

Cut the fish into strips 1½ inches (4 cm) thick and add to the other ingredients. Cover and simmer for about 6 minutes until the fish is just cooked.

Serve with fluffy boiled rice and a green vegetable.

MONKFISH LORRAINE

2 × approx. 1 lb (450 g) monkfish tails (or 2 lb/900 g fillet of huss)

2½ oz (65 g) butter or margarine

2 large onions, sliced thinly into rings

3 tablespoons (3 × 15 ml spoon) white wine or dry cider

a pinch of mixed herbs

2 heaped tablespoons (4 × 15 ml spoon) plain flour

½ pint (300 ml) milk

3 oz (75 g) grated Cheddar cheese

4 hard-boiled eggs, shelled and sliced thickly

a pinch of cayenne pepper or paprika

salt and freshly ground black pepper

Oven temperature:
Gas Mark 6/400°F/200°C

A quick and simple supper dish I am very fond of is that of thinly sliced and softly cooked onion rings with sliced hard-boiled eggs and a well-flavoured cheese sauce. So I tried the same idea incorporating a good firm-fleshed and well-flavoured fish. It was excellent.

Cut the monkfish neatly off each side of the backbone (which, by the way, doesn't have any side bones) or cut the huss into four equal lengths.

Melt 1 oz (25 g) of the butter in a shallow pan large enough to take the fish, add the onion rings and cook them over a low heat until they are soft and golden (do not allow to brown). Add the wine or cider and cook over a high heat, stirring, until the liquid is reduced by about half. Season the fish with salt and pepper and place it on the onions. Sprinkle over the herbs and cover the pan tightly. Cook over a low heat for 10 minutes.

Preheat the oven. Melt the remaining butter in a small saucepan. Add the flour and mix well. Gradually blend in the milk, stirring continuously over a medium–high heat until the sauce comes to the boil and is thick and smooth. Add two–thirds of the cheese, season with salt and pepper and stir until the cheese has melted.

Remove the fish from the onion and cooking liquid and cut it into 1 inch (2.5 cm) thick slices. Pour the onion and the cooking liquid into a baking dish, place the fish on the onions with slices of hard-boiled egg between the slices of fish. Pour over the sauce, sprinkle over the remaining cheese and then top with a small pinch of cayenne or paprika. Bake in the oven for 10 minutes until the sauce is golden brown and the fish is tender. Serve with mashed potatoes or rice and a green vegetable.

FISH FLORENTINE

2 lb (900 g) spinach

½ teaspoon (2.5 ml spoon) lemon juice

1 tablespoon (15 ml spoon) olive or sunflower oil

4 large or 8 small fillets of flat fish (Dover or lemon sole, John Dory, dabs or plaice)

2 oz (50 g) butter, plus a little extra for the baking dish

2 tablespoons (2 × 15 ml spoon) plain flour

½ pint (300 ml) milk

3 oz (75 g) grated Cheddar cheese

salt and freshly ground black pepper, grated nutmeg and cayenne pepper

Oven temperature:
Gas Mark 5/375°F/190°C

Everyone knows about Eggs Florentine; this is the same dish but with fish fillets taking the place of the eggs. It is a good dish to serve to the whole family and one that everyone seems to enjoy.

Wash the spinach well and cook in about 1½ inches (4 cm) of boiling salted water (to which a small pinch of bicarbonate has been added) for about 4 minutes, until it is tender. Drain the spinach well in a sieve, pressing out excess water. Season it with the lemon juice, oil, salt, pepper and a pinch of nutmeg and arrange it in a flat layer in a lightly buttered, shallow baking dish.

Steam the fish in a steamer over boiling water for about 5 minutes until just cooked through and remove any black skin and bones. Arrange it over the spinach. Preheat the oven.

Heat the 2 oz (50 g) butter in a saucepan, add the flour and mix well. Gradually blend in the milk, stirring continually over a medium–high heat until the sauce comes to the boil and is thick and smooth. Add 2 oz (50 g) of the cheese, season with salt, pepper and a pinch of nutmeg and stir over a medium heat for about 3 minutes, until the cheese has melted.

Pour the sauce over the fish, sprinkle over the remaining cheese and a little touch of cayenne and bake in the oven for about 15 minutes, until the dish is heated through and the top is a bubbling golden brown.

Serve with mashed potatoes and matchstick lengths of carrots cooked with butter and finely chopped parsley, mashed swedes or roast parsnips.

SOLE ALEXA

Serves 6

6–12 fillets of lemon or
Dover sole (fillets of plaice
or dabs can also be used),
with the skin removed

2 teaspoons (2 × 5 ml
spoon) lemon juice

juice of 1½ oranges and the
grated peel of 1 orange

3 leeks

2 oz (50 g) butter

2 teaspoons (2 × 5 ml
spoon) chopped capers

¼ pint (150 ml) single
cream

2 lb (900 g) potatoes, boiled
and mashed with butter, a
little milk and seasoning

salt and freshly ground black
pepper

To garnish:

tomato slices and watercress
leaves

Sole fillets with a light leek and orange sauce served on beds of potatoes.

Sprinkle the fish fillets with the lemon juice and season them with salt and pepper. Blanch the orange peel in boiling water for 1 minute and drain well. Clean and thinly slice the leeks.

Melt 1 oz (25 g) butter in a saucepan, add the leeks and cook over a low heat, stirring to prevent browning, until the leeks are soft and transparent. Add the orange juice, bring to the boil and boil for 1 minute. Lower the heat, add the capers and orange peel and gradually beat in the cream, stirring continuously over a medium–high heat until the sauce thickens. Keep warm.

Shape the mashed potato into six oblongs a little larger than the fish fillets; reheat thoroughly on a serving dish and keep warm.

Melt the remaining butter and brush the fish fillets with it. Grill under a hot grill for about 5 minutes, only until the fish is just cooked. Place the fish fillets on the potato beds, pour over the sauce and serve at once. Garnish the dish with slices of peeled, firm ripe tomatoes, topped with watercress leaves.

INDEX TO RECIPES

Design and layout: Ken Vail Graphic Design
Photography: Robert Golden
Food preparation for photography: Anne Ager,
Mary Cadogan
Stylist: Antonia Gaunt
Illustrations: John York
Typesetting: Westholme Graphics Ltd
Printed and bound by Balding & Mansell Ltd,
Wisbech, Cambs